50

8

7

6

5

4

3

2

...

8 THE ESCAPE

"8 Months to go, to the birth of the first child born, after the parent was injected with the Jagirremi Serum. The Serum that she instigated her brilliant husband to develop, for the mentally handicapped but at her orders and strange methods was injected into a highly intelligent human being and the child will be a "Brilliant". She is determined to make big money and won't stop at anything.

Pinching her eyes slightly closed against the wind made by the copter blades, Mary held her breath in the take-off. Gavin, the pilot, was actually hiding her, from the sight of those watching from the roof top. While clutching at her briefcase Mary slid down onto the skid. The landing was but a two meter drop, for her to land onto the small patio, of the 5th floor. Her heart was pounding. She knew even a couple of centimeters short, would send her plummeting down to her death. But while balancing the helicopter in one place, Gavin had given her a sign, a wink and a smile, that the time was right. She had anchored herself with the briefcase on the skid when she allowed her shoes to fall onto the patio below. It was but a fleeting moment, that Mary cringed as her gaze followed the falling shoes. They flew at a speed, hitting the stone patio and then bounced to a halt. One lay against the railing and she imagined for a second in time, that if Gavin was holding the helicopter too much to the further side, she could even, either hit the railing or miss it and plunder to the ground. Slithering down slowly, with her back held against the helicopter, she placed the briefcase to rest slightly on the skid and then while holding it again to anchor her from the wind, allowed her first leg to hang from the skid, easing too, slowly, the second leg. When in a sitting position on the skid for a few seconds, she lifted the briefcase and allowed gravity to take her and she fell.

The landing was not as difficult as she thought it may be. Having practiced it over and over. Her body was supple, she was young, and she was Mary. Having been raised by a father who pushed her to limits, that normal ones would not survive, this treatment only made her, Mary, stronger. She advised, even to herself.

And light as a tabby, she lifted herself from the patio floor to a standing position. She gave the roof a quick glance and while clutching the briefcase, pushed the slip-on into her deep pocket. Things had gone according to her plan and she disappeared into the lab.

Once she placed the briefcase from view under the desk, she sucked her finger, exclaiming.

"That was some fall and to hurt only a finger that was holding onto the briefcase of money. Wow, I deserve a medal!"

"Luckily, I know your password, Sunshine!" She laughed and broke into the privacy of Kevin's computer. When voices sounded, Mary bent down low and hid beneath the desk opening. Her heart was beating in her throat.

"Don't spoil it for me, I'm not ready to give up just yet, plenty of money to live out, first!"

While crouching, Mary clicked the catches of the briefcase open, also holding the fleshy part of her other hand, over the popping sound that the catches made. She felt for the cold of the steel revolver, that Gavin had given to her, while saying.

"Use it. No one would be able to trace the bullets back to anyone and it has a silencer on!"

She thought of Gavin, waiting for her and breathed.

"In all the months, since I have asked him to take a house on my island, just so I can have his closeness and assistance, I have discovered him to be a total angel. Was just hard when Byron was there, too!" She giggled as the nearing footsteps, faded in the passage.

Unscrewing the hard drive quickly from inside of the computer, Mary wrapped it safely and placed it into the briefcase, locking it and then on making her way to the door, said.

"More money…" she sighed.

At that very moment, she did not worry about how Gavin was going to handle the situation further but Mary laughed to herself and thought about the words her mother always reminded.

Before leaving the lab, Mary touched the gold pendant at her neck, this action sent the electronic cameras, security doors and recorders, to turn off. Through the feeder room of the animals, she went into the room housing all electricity and threw the switch up. All was in darkness now. She felt for the rain hat in her pocket, placed it onto her head, while pulling it far over her eyes. In the passage outside, though sounding still, voices were heard when she opened the door. Walking down, she held tightly onto the revolver and the briefcase. Safely within the briefcase that housed the hard drive, was the formula for the Jagirremy Serum and a vast amount of money. She tried as much as possible to tone into the dark shadows, especially when someone came too close for comfort.

It was sudden when going down the stairs and she felt a rifle sticking hard, into her back. A voice spoke in flat tone.

"Mary, what you did was unforgivable. Not only to us islanders but to the children.

What have you got in the briefcase and what are you doing in the building. What are you doing inside, when you pretended to fall outside. You're actually supposed to be dead!"

Turning her head slightly, she stopped dead. It was Jack. She heard no sympathy in his voice tone, in fact, it did not sound like him at all, now he had lost the warmth in his voice. She knew she could not charm him, or buy him and as he was holding a rifle into her back, she knew her chances with Jack at this moment, were nil. He spoke again, this time with more determination in his voice, explaining.

At that moment everything became too much and now by the stairs, Mary slipped into a strong personality and she turned on Jack. She knew that being younger and much fitter, gave her the overhand. She fell suddenly sideways, falling hard onto her shoulder and then rolling once. Her rain hat, fell and lay discarded. Within seconds of her rolling, the shot from his rifle had sounded as he pulled the trigger. Having this happen at the moment when she rolled, the bullet scraped through her left shoulder. She was bleeding and in one move, she grabbed at her pistol, pointing it at Jack. He spoke.

"Even if I die tonight, I will make sure I kill you too!" And he held the rifle, pointing at her chest, when he demanded.

"Throw down the pistol?"

She placed the pistol down on the stairs and changed into the humbling portrait of child begging for help.

"Jack, I'm so sorry, I don't know how to make this right, and this is why I'm here. I fell from the helicopter and by some miracle. I landed on the patio and now, I want to make right for what I have done wrong and if you would care to be my guiding light in doing so, I will be forever grateful!"

His eyes were dark pools of hatred while she groveled. She even went as far as to holding up her hands, in submission.

"You can take me in for arrest, I want to make right!" She soothed this humbly, even crying. Suddenly, she reached out for the pistol, rolled again once and while holding the pistol in the air, shot him. The first bullet was into the fleshy part of his upper leg and when he aimed the rifle again, she pulled the pistol trigger. The muffled sounds reigned and Jack lay still on the stairs from the chest wound. On standing up, Mary first kicked the rifle out of his reach before picking up the briefcase. The pistol again, she held so as to use it, when necessary and she fled the captivity of the building. Mary was in pain, her shoulder was still bleeding, however it was getting less and she knows it was only a scrape from the bullet. She smiled when she thought back of what exactly just happened. She felt a bit sorry for Jack but she knew it was him or her.   She stayed in the shadows and tread silently past at places where people still huddled, discussing.

"This will be the first place they will look for me!" She breathed as she passed without being noticed.   They were evacuating the kids and the people were standing in the pathways and in disbelief looked up at the helicopters hovering and landing.   They were picking up the residents of this awful island and was taking them to a military ship nearby for treatment and therapy.

The moon disappeared behind a cloud and Mary felt it was safe enough to move. She pushed the pistol into her pocket when passing a group of guards. Moving slowly in the safety of the shadows while the moonlight played hide and seek the guards spoke in excited tone.

"She fell, before our very eyes. We were standing at the top floor, she fell but the body is nowhere, to be seen!"

The evening freshness hit one, as it danced in from the sea, sending sea spray to cover the earth and moisten the air. Still keeping to the dark, her shadow stole its way, while beach sand touches her feet. Venturing toward the sound of the waves crashing against rocks, which drowned out all other sound, she moved into the safety of the night. Running a way down, along the water's edge and then turning on the torch, while holding it face up, she allowed its beams to reach for the sky.

Mary waited anxiously for the helicopter lights to appear, while Gavin's eyes scoured the coastline, just away from the building, he was slightly nervous now but the helicopter was black and the sound was muffled by the other aircraft now doing their duty.

He laughed remembering back to a big

job, he too was involved in.

"Made enough money, don't ever need to work again but it took the patience of Job, to escape. Got to go on gut feeling this time. I just don't know if that is what the girl has. Patience!"

He laughed again, while allowing his eyes to search the coastline and he gave a sigh of relief as he recognized the light of the touch.

"There you are, now that's a patient girl. She escaped!"

It was easy for Gavin to land the helicopter on the sandy beach, he had been flying a plane for so long. He knew too that he had to move fast, the lights of the helicopter could be seen from the air. Hardly had he stopped when Mary made her appearance and by first placing the briefcase into the helicopter safely, she bounced in, herself.

"My house, quick Gavin!"

When Mary reached for her jacket and pulled it on, with much pain, it set her moaning. He asked.

"Are you injured?"

"I don't think it's serious, I'll be okay! He shot me in the shoulder"

"Who?" he asked concerned.

"Jack is dead. I shot him, it was either him or me. I didn't have a chance there. Nothing at all."

At Mary and Emma's home away from the town and a bit secluded and not easy to spot at night. Emma was frantically waiting for her parents' arrival. And when Gavin arrived with her mother, even parking the helicopter on the lawn, she knew it was an emergency.

With a frown, she asked.

"What is wrong, Mom and I saw the room behind the pantry, what is going on?"

"This is the Islands pilot, Gavin!" Her

mother introduced her and carried on.

"Emma, I'll explain everything, your father needs you at his side. It is a matter of life and death, with the accident he has been in!"

Eddy chipped in now.

"I insist on going with Emma. There's a control room in your house, I saw it, and I don't believe anything, anymore!"

He stopped for a moment but Gavin butted in and explained.

"It is an emergency, her mother will look out for her!"

Eddy opened his mouth to say something but Gavin insisted.

"It's a family matter!"

Turning to Emma, Eddy confessed.

"I want to go along with you and if this man carries on, I'm going to beat the crap out of him!"

"Shh. Eddy, he is three times your size, I'll be okay, and I'm with my mom. I feel safe now and you don't have to worry at all. I'll come and tell everything when I'm back!"

She walked to him and hold him tight and whispered.

"I love you Eddy with all my heart. I have to go to my Dad he needs me now."

Some people were approaching the house so Gavin, Mary and Emma took off.

Emma had hardly closed the copter door when she felt the needle stab into the top of her leg. She did not scream, it happened too fast and unexpectedly.

She fell into the back seat while Gavin had already turned the steering of the helicopter. Eddy did not see a thing in the dark.

"What a beautiful girl you have!" Gavin breathed to Mary.

"I'm so sorry to have done that to her but it is for the best! She is carrying another fortune"

The helicopter took off into the air.

"How is she and is that safe for her?" Gavin asked while wearing a frown and half turning.

He kept his eyes glued to the syringe as Mary stabbed it into Emma's arm again.

"Perfectly safe for her. This should knock her out for a few hours, by that time, we are in Asia heading with the private plane for the Swiss mountains!" Mary assured him.

And then leaning toward Emma, Mary whispered.

"It's alright Emma, Mom's here, you'll be safe and Dad is fine!"

Now turning to Gavin, Mary asked.

"So what's the plan?"

"All on schedule, moving all as planned, as you planned, may I say, my Lady and as you said, we are on the way to get the plane on another island and then to the Swiss Alps, where Anton will meet us with the Limousine! Mary you've made a fortune out of Kevin and he knows it. He will be coming for you one or other time. You know Emma is his daughter too and after all the news and stories are all out…he'll be the one searching for his daughter and hopefully not getting you in this process."

Mary was surprised and asked.

"Getting me? How would he get me if he doesn't even know where I am?"

"Everybody has contacts everywhere…all you have to do is to ask. And the guy from the secret service, don't forget him and remember he too has a family to protect and keep safe for now."

Mary frowned.

"What are you talking about?"

Gavin smiled and said.

"Contacts."

Mary shook her head and then spoke with confidence.

"Well done to you Darling, you made things easier for me, tonight. I shall thank you the minute, we are settled!" And she giggled.

In the ride, Mary again explained to Gavin that Emma had 8 months to go for the baby to be born.

"The first baby or "brilliant" being born after one of the parents had the Jagirremi Serum!" She boasted. He will be like no other. He will have special gifts he has to discover for himself."

Gavin asked in serious tone.

"How do you know it's a boy and the Jagirremi Serum, have you got it?"

"I have it and more!" And she played with the gold locket at her neck.

She turned to him and in serious tone, accused.

"Please don't share the little you know of my story, with anyone?"

While placing his hand in front of his mouth, Gavin pretended to lock his lips, assuring that her secret is safe with him.

He adjusted the controls and said.

"They won't pick us up now anymore, so I'm flying higher, close Emma and close yourself, it gets cold up here!"

He was restless about his first love and so Eddy stayed at Emma's home.

"I'll wait right here for her!" He insisted to himself just as Kevin and David walked in.

"Where's Emma?" They asked in turn.

"They took her to see you!"

"Who took her?"

"Her mother and a man in the helicopter. He said, he was her mother's pilot!"

Staring at him now, Kevin asked.

"Did Emma get into the helicopter?"

While nodding, Eddy also added.

"He would not allow me to accompany Emma and Emma assured me that she was okay. We said good bye and they took off. I saw the lights disappeared behind the house."

At that moment Rick rushed in at the door of Kevin's house and blurted out.

"They can't find her body, Kevin!" He waited a moment before adding.

Kevin nodded.

"They won't, it's too late. She got away with another helicopter and they're probably somewhere over the ocean flying to another island and getting her private jet to go somewhere…"

How do you know about the private Jet?

"She bought it a few days before we were all kidnapped. I wanted to ask her about that, but I thought it was for a birthday present or something adventurous she planned without telling me. Well, I should've asked but now I know she would lie to anyone she met."

"Prepare yourself for this Kevin. Your hard drive has been stolen and it's Jack…"

"Jack? Oh no…"

In shock, Kevin stared at Rick, before saying.

"She had this planned to the finest detail. Did she for one moment think what she was doing to the children?"

"Sorry Kevin, I doubt if she thought or cared for anyone other than herself. I mean what about all the children?"

"Gosh, what of Emma and her baby?"

Rick stated.

"Emma is with her. Mary kidnapped Emma!"

At that moment, David informed.

"I'll be in my room if you need anything, Dad!"

Kevin nodded and David left.

"We need to go through her things in that

attic room that you discovered!"

The whole scene of Mary falling, played repeatedly in Kevin's mind. He had tried to stop his son from seeing it and held him into his embrace and David did not see. The island men were gathered around Kevin with Mary's fall. They started to leave the scene shortly. Was it in shock but David had asked Kevin a few times.

"So, it was all Mom's doing!" And Kevin had stayed quiet.

Rick started.

"Kevin, you know that Emma is pregnant with the first brilliant!" He stared at Kevin, waiting for his reaction. When Kevin looked at him, he went on.

"She can't do this to her own daughter?" Kevin blurted out.

"You also know Mary has probably

already sold the child!"

Looking disgusted now, Kevin raked his fingers through his slightly greying dark hair, before he spoke.

"I'll get Emma back…one way or the other. His mind was racing and Kevin informed Rick.

"I'm going to contact my brother. He's an advocate and let him sort out a quick divorce. Want to forget her, as fast as possible!"

Just then someone came in from the attic. Philip came in and stated.

"I've found what I need the most. Her flight plan!"

"Well count me in. I'm going to help you find her and bring her to justice!" Kevin stated adamantly.

"I'm in too, just let me know where and when!" Rick added before he greeted and left.

Alone, Kevin sat in the comfy chair in the lounge and into the dark night, he cried into his hands. It was then, that at another's earlier suggestion,

Chrystal appeared in Kevin's doorway, she insisted.

"I'm not leaving you?"

He nodded, asking.

"Where are Jack's kids?"

"In any case even when Jack's home, they love my brother and his wife to bits. They're always there!"

In the dark until late the evening, Chrystal sat by Kevin. It was only when he reached his hand out to her saying.

"Let's go to bed?"

That she rose and joined him.

Still not making sense of what had happened, it was a relief to Kevin not anymore needing to work on the escape plan of taking the Islanders and leaving the island to be safe. He and Chrystal lay side by side, just holding hands, while Kevin's thoughts, never for one moment stopped.

It was high tide and the water reached

almost to the pathway, after the garden. The air smelled of salt and mist on a warm coastal night. The waves never stopped rushing for the shore not even for a moment, endlessly sounding, throwing out treasures and taking in what it could lay its churning waters on.

On the third story of Kevin's home, it felt as if his world had tumbled and tonight here in his bed, now lay the women, he had loved with every beat of his young heart. A woman who had the same interests as he did, the woman who he dreamed of sharing a lifetime with. How does one condition a mind that has been married for so long, as to not feeling guilty, of two timing your husband? Deep in his heart, Kevin played to rid himself of the guilt that could steal his happiness. Chrystal started telling him that she had known Mary's story, for a long time and was not at liberty to talk about it, he felt better, knowing that she understood. They lay and spoke of their student days and things, they got up to. He had to admit.

"You know I feel alive again, being with you. And this time, I ask again.

"Will you Chrystal…?"

She knew the question and her face was serious and full of admiration and love.

"Yes, I will marry you!"

They fell asleep in each other's embrace and long before dawn Chrystal dressed and left saying.

"I think until David is over everything and can handle a new shock, we'll keep our feelings under the lid!"

"I need to buy you an engagement ring with pearls and diamonds!"

"Oh, Kevin you remembered. Wow!"

"Off course I remember. You will always be my first love, Chrystal!"

At the door she turned back and whispered.

"My taste has changed though. I want only diamonds now!"

Kevin nodded and winked one eye.

Smiled and said.

"Then plenty of diamonds it will be!"

It was later in the morning when a helper brought the children home on this Sunday from sleeping over, he walked into Jack's home and called.

"When I left Uncle Kevin's house to go to yours, our house was still in darkness. Dad has not been home, yet!"

The lifesavers boat was still at the same spot as Kevin had left it.

"And the ferry is not here!"

"The only place Jack could be now is at the Wikita Island!"

At the work Island, in the reception area, Kevin pressed 5 for a lift!"

He thought for a moment and added.

"The mains are off!" He stared at Rick before he insisted.

"Let's walk!"

It was on the third floor that Jack's body

lay against the stairs. Rick bent down to feel for a pulse.

Kevin spoke.

"Death was almost instantaneous, telling by the open eyes and the position, he is lying in!"

Bending down now, Kevin spoke all the while.

"Another fact is that rigor mortis has already set in. The bullet could not have missed his brain and that in itself could have been fatal. See the fleshy part of the body is in the shape to the stairs and positioning around it, showing that he died right here. The body was not moved. But I would say, considering the temperature here in the stairway, we could work out the exact time of death. I can also see post mortem stain, forming at the buttocks and back, that from the blood not moving in the body!" He gave his eyes a wipe and added.

"We have to get a guard and get Jack in for a post mortem!"

"Oh Shit, not one guard!" Rick explained, asking.

"Do you think this is Jack's rain hat?"

"That's Mary's hat, I know it well!" Kevin insisted.

"I'll get a sheet from my lab and we can close him until we can find someone to help us!"

It broke Kevin's heart to have to tell the children that their father had been deceased but having a home they loved and already waiting, made it easier. For Kevin to just know that Chrystal was there for them and for him too, it made things even easier. The kids were devastated about Jack and they were comforted by Chrystal. She made sure the kids were fine and Kevin started to make arrangements for Jack's funeral. It was in two days and they had to go back to his home town to bury him. The kids knew there was a special place where he wanted to be buried.

Emma

32

It was after the luxurious private plane ride that on riding on the helicopter, belonging to Gavin, that Emma came fully to and saw, on looking down, the beauty of the snow clad world, beneath her. She drew in her breath and in soft tone, let out.

"Oh my soul, this is too beautiful to be possible. Where are we?"

It was Mary, sitting next to her, that informed her wearing a soft smile and using a soft tone of voice. Nearly lovable.

"You're awake, you and I are on our way, going on holiday to the Swiss Alps remember, Emma. You fell and bumped your head!"

Turning slightly, Gavin stared at Emma, smiling before he started explaining.

"We are travelling over the Swiss Plateau now. The region you are seeing is the Mont Blanc area and we share this beauty with countries like Liechtenstein, Austria, France and Germany. My cabin is situated in the sub Alpine zone, it is just beneath the tree level. The peaks consist of flowers and small shrubs higher up, well that is when they are not under snow. Lower down, one finds the tree level, where forests of beauty adorn the mountains and then the lower level is the level where houses and towns are built. As you will see, we that are in the Mont Blanc area, have continuous overhangs of snow, that accumulate above toward the mountain peaks.

At this moment, for Mary, admiration shone through her eyes when looking at Gavin, he was of big build with blondish hair, blue green eyes and a strong chin. He smiled often and Mary wished that she could put her hand out and touch the cleft in his chin. She wanted to say to him.

"It's your smile that attracts me the most, your open personality, your charm, your big build. Oh, I don't know, it's just everything about you that I love and cannot wait to get hold of and have you for myself!"

But Emma was with them and the time

was not right. The planes intercom started.

"Come in Gavin, do you read me?"

He stayed cool, all the while smiling, even when he put the intercom at his leisure, to his lips, saying.

"Hi ya Cindy, how's my girl?"

She sounded excited, when she said.

"I'm not hearing from you, how close are you to landing?"

"I'm just readying to land at the cabin. Got the guests with me!"

To Mary it was as if he was giving some message because Cindy's voice sounded less excited and she guided him to stand still. When the plane stopped, Gavin jumped out and opened the door for Mary, also helping Emma out. He introduced them to the friendly and motherly woman who came first to meet them and help with luggage.

"This is my right hand Mrs. Schutzler. She sees that everything in the home runs according to clockwork!"

Fleetingly the young women pressing out pie dough, looked up, waved and looked away. He introduced her.

"And this is Anton. He does everything, no one else is doing. He is the son to me I never had!"

Everyone laughed and Gavin ordered.

"Anton would you give me a hand in getting our guests baggage to their rooms!"

It was Mrs. Schutzler that suggested.

"Mary shall we go inside for some tea and home baked biscuits?"

While approving the invitation, Mary turned to Gavin and asked.

"Would you be okay getting Emma to her bedroom, Sweetie?" She stared at him and explained.

"With the fall, her balance might be out!"

Inside the house, Mary looked around and could not hide her surprise.

"Wow Mrs. Schutzler, I would never have dreamed the place is so spacious!"

The older woman with pride announced.

"Five bedrooms Mary, my Gavin, he is like a son to me, enjoys his luxury. Sometimes we have many guests over!"

Joining them now, Gavin asked Mrs. Schutzler.

"Can I steal our guest away from you?"

And he turned to Mary for a moment and gave her a wink. He informed Mrs. Schutzler.

"As I already told you, Mary and Emma will be staying for a few months, I hope you will enjoy the company I have brought you!"

He then turned to Mary again and suggested.

"A quick tour of the home, so you know your way around!" He then stopped, pulled her to the lounge and went on to say.

"But first!"

In the massive space of the lounge, among the chunky pure leather furniture, he pulled her to him and kissed her, whispering.

"I've missed you and have dreamed of

this day!”

She placed her arms around his neck and while standing on tiptoes, whispered.

“This is life. Thank you Gavin!”

When she pulled away, she stated.

“I have to check up on Emma!”

He held her hand and led her to the bedroom while he at the door whispered.

“Not going in!”

She smiled and said.

“Thanks Gavin, thanks for understanding!”

In the huge bedroom, the temperature was warm and Emma lay against the embroidered pillows.

“You look like a real live Snow White!” Mary touched her forehead and she opened her eyes, asking.

“I don’t know why I cannot for the life of me remember anything?”

“Everything’s fine Emma. You fell and knocked your head. We were going away for a bonding holiday for about six months.

"Dad and David?" she asked

Dad and David are all well, at home. Eddy's fine too!"

She could not help but wonder that Emma did not ask about the baby and Mary promised herself not to mention it.

While not saying much, except.

"My head aches!" Emma stayed in bed.

"It's from the fall!"

Mary fussed around her, keeping her happy, also suggesting.

"For the change in climate, we will have to go out and get a few warm things. I see Gavin has bought the basics. Let me know as soon as you are feeling strong enough, for us to take the trip into town?"

"Who is Gavin?"

"Did you never meet the Island pilot? When he told me that he had a cabin in the Swiss Alps, I thought it would be good for you and I, to do some bonding and I booked it, immediately!"

Emma nodded and snuggled into the blanket, saying.

"It's so great just being here in this room, on our holiday!"

There was a knock at the door and it opened before anyone could reply.

"You both must be starving, I've brought breakfast!"

"Oh, Mrs. Schutzler this is my daughter Emma. Emma meet Mrs. S.

"I'm so please to meet you in this beautiful surroundings."

She is like a mother to Gavin and in charge of the running of the household!"

Sitting upright now, Emma smiled and said.

"Oooh, now I am starving. Glad to meet you Mrs. S.!"

A while later, she stretched lazily when her tray was taken.

"Gee Mom, Bacon on French pancakes with lashings of syrup are just what the doctor ordered. That was really something!"

"Well Emma, if were supposed to bond and enjoy a holiday at the same time, the best is not good enough for my girl!"

Grinning now, Emma lay back down and said.

"I'm tired and I'm going to sleep for a while. Please wake me up in two to three hours. Mary let her be. She knows the special gift she carried and she must make sure Emma will deliver the baby boy without complications.

About three hours later…Mary walked in and found Emma dressed up and ready to go.

Mary exclaimed

"Wow, you don't take no for an answer…I know you and then let's go."

"Well, let the day begin!"

She did hold onto her head within a minute though but decided to bear it.

"Are you okay, Emma?" Mary was concerned.

"I'm fine Mom and it's so great to be here

with you in this absolute beautiful place. You've been planning this for long?"

The question caught Mary by surprise but she sighed and smiled and said.

"For you my darling I will give you the world as a gift."

"Thanks Mom, love you lots."

In the cabin lounge, a fire was going, leaving the temperature to be quite comfortable. Mrs. S. brought in a tray with hot chocolate and Gavin thanked her. Being all cuddled up in a thick warm clothes for the outing, left Emma sitting peacefully and content.

"Mom, where are we going first?"

"Even Dad and David, I don't miss them too much, but on the other hand this holiday, can't miss a moment here!"

Sitting in a chair opposite Gavin was his right hand man, Anton. Staring past the cup of hot chocolate she was holding, Emma stole a glance at the well-built but tall,

Anton, she loved the way he wore his dark untamed hair, long and tied back. His facial features were softened slightly when his naturally curly thick hair, fell down his back, like she had seen him earlier.

"Geez he is yummy. Can one be so divine?" She wondered and got angry for not thinking about Eddy. Eddy…remember.

Gavin noticed Emma staring at Anton and informed with a mischievous smile, playing.

"This young man is of Sioux roots and I just cannot find a way to get him to cut off his hair!"

Giving a small laugh, Anton amplified.

"Boss, where in my contract does it say that I have to wear my hair like you want me to?"

"Oh, I just never thought of putting in that clause, actually I did not know you even have a contract!"

This sent them into laughter.

"If Anton has to cut his hair, I'm going to shave my own off!" Emma thought.

It was as if everyone stared at her beautiful strawberry blonde hair, which fell thick over her shoulders, before letting a roar of laughter break out.

"No, no don't you have amazing hair!" They cried.

Mary was heard saying.

"And where on this heaven's earth do you spring from Emma, I'm sure Anton is big enough, to fight his own battles?"

Anton's eyes met with Emma's and she blushed.

His boss while wearing a grin, commented.

"Mmmmm. Anton!"

This sent Emma to hide her face, while giggling, saying.

"I did not mean it like that?"

Turning to stare at her suddenly, Anton pretended to look disappointed now, asking her.

"I thought you are on my side. How did you mean it then, please explain?"

She looked deeply into his dark, dangerous

eyes, they drew her to him and her heart was beating like an untamed drum and Eddy's profile came into her mind and she said.

"Sorry boy, I'm taken."

Mary started to laugh out loud and said.

"Emma, we should get going. The world awaits."

The door opened and Mrs. S walked into the room and announced.

"Supper is ready!"

At the table while Mrs. S., Anton, Dina, Emma, Mary and Gavin were seated, Gavin said grace and shocked Mary, by giving thanks for the family seated at his table.

"Shall we do a bit of shopping today?"

Gavin asked, while searching the faces before him and then he enquired.

"You Emma, I did not get you a warm coat, I left it till you got here!"

He felt comfortable, Gavin knew where a woman's soft spot lay and used this technique and it worked.

"Oh, that will be glorious Uncle Gavin, thanks!"

And when alone, he pulled Mary to him and informed.

"I shall see you at 11 tonight in the warmth of your bed!"

She had lifted her half open lips, awaiting his touch. Mary was content.

They drove with the car to town and the town was like a sweet from heaven and Emma enjoyed every little shop and when she asked, Mary produced her card and paid the bill."

With lots of little bags they returned and Emma went to her room to enjoy her beautiful gifts. One was something special. A glass figure of a horse running in the wind.   She hold it in her hands and whispered softly. Eddy I love you with all my heart. This was her way of never forgetting Eddy. Never. She vowed that she will stay loyal, no matter what. She stayed in her room until dinner and then she decided to go to sleep…meanwhile…

It was late night, he sat quietly staring into the fire, and Gavin was a happy man. He loved people and loved to make sure that the ones closest, were comfortable. He did not need much himself, besides the solitude of life here in the cabin. He listened as a far cry of a wolf in the nature reserve sounded. Taking in the sound, drinking it in, as if it were a tonic, he closed his eyes, while in the hearth the coals burned, cracked and shot tiny cinders, in the glow of the heat. He had loved Mary from the first day that he saw her but knew in his heart that she would never be his. He did not only know of her husband but also the lovers that filled her life with amusement. He still know a few but one comes to mind immediately. Andre…
Now on his life path, she had become a part but for how long, he did not know. Not being an opportunist, or even a shark,

Gavin was going to be there for her until she again decided, as she had in her marriage to Kevin, to move on. He pushed it from his mind and listened as the thin air on the outside of the cabin brought sounds from far, carrying them clearly on its crispness. He whispered.
"I love the lonely call of the wolf!"
A loud crack of ice sounded from high, as ice fingers that hung from cliffs far above, took their course, snapped and sent the discarded spikes to slither, to the ground.

Since the shooting of Jack, the children had fitted in living with another couple and they were Philip and Magda. They took Jack's death with much more heart ache than Veronica's. Their mother who they had lost, had been the cause of them to become totally dependent on their father, but he now was also gone.

"He died within moments of the shot. She had pointed the pistol to reach the most vital part of the brain. He did not have to bear any pain!" Kevin had assured.

Chrystal was around for the children to council them and this made understanding death, more bearable. The children all missed him and Magda and Chrystal's brother, Philip were both grateful for a family of their own. Kevin and Chrystal too stayed very involved in their lives, especially as communication on the island was now allowed and the previous horrid rules, when Mary was in control of the island, had fallen away. A board was appointed and the Muni-landers organized their lives so as to carry on living, making this still their home, but now in pleasant circumstances. It was not long when Philip and Kevin were talking and Philip disclosed.

"I have a lead where Mary could have gone, but I actually want to suggest that we give her time to get tame. When she thinks that we are not after her anymore, she will make mistakes!"

"I have a couple of dollars to spare, I say I back you and when the time is right, and we find her, Philip!"

Thinking for a moment, before Kevin also carried on to say.

"The sake of me finding my Emma for the sake of her unborn child, is reason enough. And for the sake of the Jagirremy Serum and the good it can do for the world, I say, we have more than enough reason, to find her. Anywhere in the world, where you think she may be. I'll be ready to be there with you at any time!" Kevin promised.

"We will keep a look out for her!" Philip, a member of the FBI promised.

For Emma, this holiday was a dream come true. The island and the hardship there was, was the furthest thing from her mind. She woke this morning and they were all going shopping with Uncle Gavin. Her heart gave a little lurch when she thought of Anton. She thought of his hair and tried to imagine what it would feel like to have his lips on hers. She caught herself while still in bed, with face upturned and lips slightly parted, pretending what it would be like.

"To be so close, that I can feel his breath on me!" She whispered as her hand gently played with a curl of her own hair.

Smitten by Anton, when he helped Emma into the helicopter, for a moment their eyes locked and she knew, he felt something. She blushed slightly, thought about the glass horse and moved further away. She wondered about Anton as well and one moment when their eyes lingered and his lips held her captive. For some reason that she never even thought about, or understood, Emma was confused and thought about Eddy. She thought of the wonderful times at the waterfall…

In the helicopter, Gavin turned the helicopter slightly to its side and spoke.

"Emma that is our nearest town and the community are proud that it is so picturesque. Even have postcards with photos of it on!"

"Uncle Gavin I'm in awe, I have never seen such beauty in all by life. Just the snow laden pines and the white mountains and all the cabins, it's just wow!"

She stopped for a moment and then said.

"I just have not seen another cabin the size of yours, Uncle Gavin!"

He laughed and answered her, by saying.

"It's a blessing Emma, to live in it!"

Having stayed quiet did not mean that Mary was discontented. In her mind she went through the evening with Gavin, over and over. It felt good to be away from the last months of stress and now in the middle of no-where not to be found, was divine.

Mary did not even think of Kevin and when something came up that she had to remember anything of yesterday, she was even irritable. What she saw in Gavin's eyes was enough for her and she wanted it with everything, she had. She wanted Gavin, he seemed to have a contentment that she, Mary, just somehow could not yet, possess. Mary loved Gavin and yes, she needed him with everything inside of her.

Thinking back to the morning hours, he had loved her without holding back. In fact he had loved her like she wanted to be loved. A niggling feeling warned her that she could not possess him, like she had possessed Kevin but she pushed it from her mind.

"Is that why I want him so much. Is he so out of my reach to keep, is that why I want him so very much?"

In her mind Mary carried on wondering.

"And Emma, will she get over Eddy? And

the medication that I used on Emma definitely caused memory loss, but will that stay. Emma is really fine as she is, thinking this is a long holiday!"

The guys waited for the girls to finish their shopping and this made Emma feel more important, more grown up and more bonded with her mother, Mary. Stealing glances of Anton every now and again, caused Emma a radiance that brought out her true and natural beauty. Anton's eyes never left her for a moment. Mary helped her buy a few pieces of clothing and not once did the feeling or the conversation come up that Emma was pregnant.

They lunched at a very unique restaurant and by the time the four were back in the helicopter, it was as if they had been a family for years. When Anton reached out and took Emma's hand in his, she let go. She felt she belonged, not there, but she wished this holiday would never end.

It was after being exactly a month in the

Swiss Alps, here in the cabin, which Mary and Gavin had left that afternoon, taking Mrs. S for shopping in town. A blizzard had come up when the phone rang in the cabin. Anton answered and came back saying.

"The folks are staying over in town, the weathers turned nasty and there's too much risk in coming home now!"

Anton packed a good fire and Emma fetched a thick quilt and pillows and there they watched DVD's for hours as the logs crackled and glowed.

"It's like watching elves and goblins at play in the fireplace!" Emma enthused this and later while lying comfortably close to Anton, he turned towards her and wanted to kiss her. Emma knew that she loved Eddy, but while his hair hung loose over his shoulders and in the firelight his skin glowed, bronze. Emma put her fingers to his lips, touching them lightly.

"You're beautiful, Anton!"

In his slight accent, he asked.

"Is this not what I'm supposed to say to you?"

She giggled and said.

"I'm serious Anton, you are the most beautiful thing that has ever happened to me!"

He spoke in broken English.

"I do not know that when women say I am beautiful, what I'm supposed to say. You can help me. Yes?" He teased her.

Swiping at him with her flat hand, made Emma squeal with laughter. She asked.

"Don't women tell you, you are beautiful, all the time? I bet they do and I'm not the only one…"

"I stay here with Dina who has a boyfriend and Mrs. S. who can be my mother. No women to say these things to me. You, you say!"

Emma was giggling now and through it all, she was trying to instruct him.

Staring at him, she waited for his

reaction. He took rather long, before saying.

"It's too complicated, I'd rather just come home to you. You not going back to Island home again. Okay, now you stay here. You now belong to Anton!"

"First repeat what I just told you?"

"You not to say that I'm beautiful to me, I belong Emma now!"

Emma was laughing with delight, even when he started kissing her in her neck which send chills throughout her body and with the fire cracking, shooting cinders and giving off luscious warmth, on a snowy night, in the chill of the Swiss Alps. They did not do anything other than talk through the night. Anton told of his mother who was an American European and of his father, who was the Indian chief.

"And when he was killed, I took my mother and we started a new life in America. There, I looked after her until she was laid to rest!"

"How did your father pass away?"

"When the cold comes to take over, the Indian Chief and his men go to warmer places and hunt buffalo, to bring back for the winter. I was but a young man trained by my father and the men of the tribe to stand in for the chief, someday. When we were on our journey the Apache tribe, caught us unexpectedly, where we were meeting around the fire, peacefully discussing the following days travel. They, the Apache are a ruthless tribe and went out of their way to kill the chief. I loaded my arrow, like father had taught me and when I aimed, all I had in my mind was that their chief had shot my father through the heart. He, the Apache chief, had mounted his horse to get away, but I killed him while still facing me. Now in our tradition, I was supposed to take over my father's place as chief, especially as I now already had a feather for the head gear, of a chief. We mourned for my father and I helped my mother to plant a purple moonflower at the waterfall, near where we buried him. That flower that blooms by the waterfall was her way of saying goodbye to him. I knew for the sake of her safety, I needed to offer up my roots and take her to the American civilization, her roots!"

It was at dawn when Emma woke, wondering if she should make for her bedroom or just lay as if dead, before he awoke. But on turning, she looked into his eyes. He lay perched on one elbow, while staring at her.

"What are you looking at?" She asked, while holding her hand before her face.

"You're beautiful!"

"I've just woken and have no make-up on!" She squealed.

When Anton in the early morning light, placed her hand on his heartbeat, saying.

"You see my heart beats stronger now.

"Put on very warm snow clothes, were going out!"

"Out where!"

"Just out!"

When they arrived outside, Anton carried the basket and held her hand. Emma was giggling.

"These snow shoes take a degree to walk in!"

He stared down at the shoes for a moment and then bent down, demanding.

"Lift your foot!"

And he swept her to sit on his bent knee. She screeched with laughter.

"I'm going to fall!"

He took the snow shoes and exchanged feet while announcing.

"That should be much better!"

She was blushing now.

"Darn, I had them on the wrong way!"

While still kneeling on one knee in the snow and while she was safely perched thereon, he held her to him and kissed her. Emma threw her arms around his neck when he whispered.

"My Darling!"

Emma drew back and said.

"No, this is wrong."

While helping her down from his knee, he held onto her hand steadying her all the while and then rose himself, picked up the basket of food.

"Where are we going?"

"You'll see!" He replied, wearing a smug smile.

Pulling him to stop a moment, Emma put her hands to her mouth. He followed her gaze to where a few squirrel were at play.

"They are so sweet!" She breathed, also asking.

"Don't you love the innocence in their eyes?"

"I do and the way they sit and stare at one. Look at that one holding the nut!" He whispered.

"I want one!" She insisted.

"They are happiest in nature, leave them to be, beautiful?"

The scenery was magnificent, walking in the wonderland of snow and pines. The air was fresh and clear and one felt as though you would be able to see into eternity. The skies were blue and being with Anton made it even more beautiful.

"Panting already, shall we stop and rest, Emma?"

"No, I'll be okay, have we far to walk?"

Anton pointed a short way ahead at a smoking chimney and disclosed.

"I asked the domestic lady to prepare the cabin for us, for a picnic!"

"My gosh, that sounds amazing!"

Emma also added.

"I would not have even known that there was a cabin in sight!"

He held onto her hand and demanded at the front door of the small cabin.

"Let us go down the stairs, be careful here is much snow, I'm sure you need a rest now!"

She looked radiant from the fresh air and the walk and exclaimed.

"Oh Anton this is magnificent inside here, do you keep it for some specific reason?"

"When Gavin walks, he likes to be alone sometimes, "closer to the wild" as he states and he has guests staying over here sometimes. It is also just in case of an emergency!"

She stared at him and he explained.

"When there are climbers and something happens, a place to overnight is needed!'

He bent down and kissed her before he asked. She followed…thought about the horse and said to herself…a holiday with a difference.

"Where would you like to eat, in front of the fire or in the cozy bedroom?"

"This place is so dreamy, even with the fireplaces, I can't make up my mind, you decide!"

"First I want you to see the bedroom!"

Her mouth hung open wide, to see the

magnificence, as if some bride were spending her wedding night. Petals of flowers lay strewn, it smelled of lemons and lavender. She could not get out a sound but eventually with a sparkle in her eyes, admitted.

"I have never seen such magnificence, wow, I just love it!"

She also exclaimed.

"Oh my gosh. Swiss chocolate, a basketful of Swiss chocolate!"

He took a handful of chocolates and placed them down next to the bath. And then while fidgeting at the music station, he put on some soft music. He fidgeted with the taps and had the water running. They got out and went to bed.

In awe Emma stated.

"I wish we could just lie in bed in this atmosphere forever!"

"I wish I could give you that wish, forever!" And he started to kiss her and she kissed him back.

It was much later when he disappeared into the kitchen and brought in a tray, even a vase, with a tiny bunch of violets on it.

"Ooh, yummy, I love smoked Gammon!"

It was by midday when he reminded.

"I think we should be getting back, I have not heard the helicopter so the folks aren't back yet!"

"Ah, I wish this could never have ended!"

"We'll do this often, I promise you!"

It was one morning long after that, when Emma asked Mary.

"Mom when are we leaving to go back home?"

The devious mother played her games, saying.

"I'm just not in the mood for all those rules and limitations yet!"

That was the moment Emma, decided to talk to her.

"Mom, Anton and I are in love!"

Mary was shaken. She had not planned

this and wondered.

"What the hell now?"

Emma also added.

"I think I am pregnant!"

"Oh heaven, Emma!" Mary started.

"I'm sorry Mom!" She started to cry and finished.

"I'm sorry, I've disappointed you!"

"Oh Emma, don't get me wrong, it is not you, I never realized, I mean!"

"Emma I'm so happy!"

It was just then when Anton came looking for Emma.

"Sweetheart, where are you?"

He saw that she had been crying and he turned to Mary,

"Mrs. Ross please if anyone is to blame, it is me, and Emma is not to blame!"

"Anton, it could have happened to anyone. Love happens all the time. But congratulations, I believe you are going to be father one of these days!" He was proud. Anton was proud and he added.

"I will be able to look well after your daughter and my child, Mrs. Ross, I will!"

"I know, thank you!" Mary heard herself saying this, before she fled to the bathroom.

"What the hell now. What do I do now, with more complications? He's thinking, he's the father. The child has been sold and I need the money!' Mary cried, while admitting.

"One lie upon the next and now I have to live with this. What am I going to say to Gavin?"

Whilst patting her face dry, Mary claimed.

"Well, in for a penny, in for a pound. I'll steal the child, if I have to!"

At the table within the confines of the log cabin, there was much excitement and Anton and Emma were the center of the attraction or excitement. Gavin fetched a bottle of very dated wine, stating as he put down the small bottle of orange juice.

"And that is for the mother and my grandchild!"

"Oh yes, mother of my child, there will be nothing that could do my child any harm, touching your lips, please!" Anton stated this proudly.

With a glint of laughter playing in his eyes, Gavin looked quietly content to all around, but he was actually wondering.

"For how long will I keep Mary this satisfied and have her with me?"

The snow had hardly melted from the lower part of the mountains when Anton and Emma became engaged. It was a quiet celebration but the friends of Gavin and Anton sent gifts and well wishes. Feeling radiant and as if standing on the edge of the Universe, Emma welcomed this baby, the fruit of the love, she felt for Anton and Eddy still in the background. Anton is the proud father never doubted for one moment that Emma loved him with everything she could love him with. When Anton left to go anywhere, he would leave her with these words.

"Take care of you and our little one, my love!" And she did.

When going for a walk one fine midday, Emma declared.

"Uncle Gavin, I'm fascinated that as the snows are melting they are exposing flowers beneath where once it looked like only snow was!"

"Nature is a wonderful thing Emma. And here where one least expects it, you discover the most treasured of nature!"

"Oh, look a deer!" Emma pointed out.

It was only when Mrs. S. called them for supper that they started walking toward the cabin.

"Brr!" Emma amplified, adding.

"I'm so glad to be inside, it is so warm and homely, a real home to come home to!"

That night when Emma went to bed, she lay listening to the call of a lonely wolf in the nature reserve nearby. An owl screeched nearby and she leaned forward pulling the curtain back and allowing the moonlight to reach onto her bed. She saw the glass horse…

When she closed her eyes, she dreamed of a waterfall and swimming in the clear of it.

"Approximately 7 months to the birth of the first "Brilliant" child, born after the father, had the Jagirremi Serum injection. Grow baby grow, when I sell Emma's baby, I'm rich!" Mary breathed, while showing herself off, in the full length mirror.

Within the month after their arrival in Switzerland, Gavin was preparing the helicopter to take Mary and Emma to be picked up by her client, at the central airfield. Gavin gave a wolf whistle, before saying.

"Wow. You look stunning. Sure you're going for business?"

He had never experienced jealousy and wondered if this situation would have set off such a feeling within a man that had known, what Mary was capable of. He wondered.

"Kevin for instance, did he ever feel jealous of having this beautiful wife and wondering if he is sharing her, with anyone else?"

Dressed in a tight fitting red top and black tailor cut slacks, Mary threw her arms around Gavin and disclosed.

"I am going to be faithful to you for the rest of my life, Gavin. You may as well get used to it!"

It was Gavin who spoke, saying to Mary.

"Are you sure you know the persons picking you up. And if you are going to be back within a week, I want you to arrange, so I know to be here for you at the airfield!"

She had turned to him and with every move she made, her perfume filled his nostrils. He stated.

"I love that smell!"

"Gavin, stop being a worry. I have business to attend to and the moment I am finished, I will let you know to fetch me at central airfield again!"

When she had a moment alone with Gavin before leaving, she held him close and said.

"I love you Gavin and you better stay faithful to me!"

Gavin wore a broad smile. He shook his head and laughed.

"You, always!" He declared and went on.

"You are the one that needs to be staying faithful to me!"

And when she was safely in the luxury craft of her client, Anton turned to Gavin and their eyes understood, just what each was thinking.

When having decided that Mary was doing this trip, Anton insisted as always to be by the side of Gavin and when Gavin turned the helicopter slightly, leaving the two girls in the safety of the plane still on the ground, it was Anton who waved and blew an unseen kiss at Emma, where she peeped longingly from the window.

On reaching their destination in France, Mary and Emma were taken in a black Mercedes, accompanied by two other Mercedes of body guards, to the Sbibvon Chateau. Once inside the building, they were shown to a luxury suite on the top landing. The furniture and draping's were of French design and the lacquered luxury was light and costly. When standing alone, outside on the small balcony, Mary drank in the flickering of city lights. They stretched as far as the eye could see, blinking, drawing one closer to their midst. The lights made a wondrous display around the Eiffel Tower, which stood upholding, pointing, reaching, embracing, and even ruling, drawing one into the mystery hidden within the heavens.

"Brrr!" Mary complained and went inside, shutting out the light chill and locking the door.

She drew the drapes, and set the purring

air conditioner, up. Then setting up the DVD player and placing the DVD down next to it, gave Mary a feeling of satisfaction, as to calming her nerves, for the coming up interview. She whispered.

"Tomorrow at two in the afternoon, I shall see you in the boardroom and I'll be a rich woman, rid of the Jagirremi and the brilliant will be in safe, caring hands!"

On the island, life fell into a relaxed and happy way for the Islanders and also the influx of the holiday makers that had started coming in and enjoying the carefree experience and absolute beauty, that one feasted their eyes on here. Jack's children Jackie, Carrie and Eddy, had been staying with Philip and Magda for a month and they had now nagged Philip on this late afternoon, into taking a walk with them. At the Ross house, Philip enthused.

"Kevin, the children convinced me to take a leisurely walk with them, around the island. Oh, I agreed on condition, that the walk should include a stop off, to see how you are doing and here we are!"

Kevin laughed and his mind went back to Alicia and the way she could turn him around her small finger. He remembered back to the day, they went fishing. He remembered too that Mary instructed her not to eat the fin fish but to eat the chicken that she had specially made for Alicia. Kevin remembered holding Alicia, while she was dying. He kept thinking that it could have been from the mercury in the fish and the allergy, when it was the Jagirremi Serum, that contained mercury as Mary had instructed her men, to be added. For a moment Kevin held the gaze of Philip, while he enthused.

"Phil, we sometimes don't appreciate the children, enough!"

Philip started to say.

"One of my men has a lead on Mary. I told you, she will get tame and think were not watching her, anymore!"

He stared at Kevin for a moment before he blurted out.

"France!"

"Does she never stop her devious ways?"

"I don't know how you held her down, for so long!" But Philip added.

"Chrystal and I will stop by later, we can talk and we can ask Magda if the children can stay over until we get back!" Kevin put in, while trying to still his heart that was beating like a drum. After all she had been his wife for so long. But he quickly thought of Chrystal, his first love and the goodness between them and he knew, he was with the one, he should have been with, since the beginning.

That evening when arriving at Philip and Magda, Rick was already there when Kevin and the children arrived. The children were elated for an evening with Jack's children and disappeared into the T.V. room.

"Take a seat, Kevin!" Philip invited before he started talking.

"And so we have a lead on Mary. Where she is hiding or has been hiding, has been a good hideout because my men are good and we did not in the full month, pick up anything on her!" he stopped took a deep breath but carried on to say.

"Now I invited Rick to join us, as I will be monitoring the whole situation from here and Rick and you, Kevin, will be keeping in close contact with me in your every move. I want to know her every move. My men all over the world too, will be keeping a close watch out for and on Mary, she will not slip through our fingers again!"

Philip stared at Rick first, before suggesting.

"Rick this might come as a terrible shock to you and I want to allow you the freedom of refusing this job, there will be plenty of other jobs, if you don't feel up to this one. The shock of this job is that, we know now that Mary is the mystery women in your son, Byron's life. Mary was his mistress!"

Rick turned his gaze to the floor but within a minute stated.

"Kevin I apologize to you and if it is okay with you, I'm in. I have suspected for a while that it is Mary and knowing who the woman is, makes it much easier now!"

Reaching out his hand to Rick, Kevin shook hands and turned back to listen to what Philip had to say.

"So we know Mary is in France, we just don't know where. She travels light but is continually doing shopping. Her need for shopping sends her radar for safety, totally out!"

The room was filled with laughter now. Philip went on to say.

"So I present to you, Kevin and to you Rick, an aircraft ticket and hotel bookings, to go pick her up. I suggest you check your firearm licenses, passports and visas and whatever else, you'd need!"

He stayed quiet now as if waiting for something.

They gave each other a quick glance, Chrystal had tears in her eyes, which sent Kevin first shifting uneasily in his chair, before he started.

"I'm going no-where without Chrystal. I will see to it that she gets the necessary travel documents, I'll get Mary at some time but I'm not leaving Chrystal again!"

Philip burst out laughing now and held up the ticket for Chrystal.

"Sorry, I had to get my Sis back, for something!"

Kevin pulled her to him, saying.

"Was not going to be without you ever again!" and kissed her.

"Paris here we come!" Chrystal breathed while they were walking on the safe part of the runway, toward the plane.

"You sure have enough clothes packed!" Kevin insisted.

"A women's priority, get used to it!"

In the taxi to the hotel, her head bobbed from side to side as she tried to drink in Paris. She kept saying.

"Oh my soul, this place is awesome!"

And when she saw the Gothic Notre-Dame Cathedral, Chrystal pointed while not saying a word.

"Is it not stunning?"

"Geez look at all those steps!"

"422 steps to be exact, Kevin!" Rick put in.

They arrived in time for a breakfast of croissants and strong coffee at the hotel Sbibvon Chateau. When Chrystal saw the Eiffel Tower from afar, she exclaimed.

"Oh my gosh, but that thing is big!"

Rick laughed aloud saying.

"Did you think it was just a model when you saw it in pics?"

"No. But seeing it in real life, well its breathtaking!"

"Do you know it weighs just over 10,000 tons?" Rick put in.

"You're joking!" Chrystal insisted and as she had not slept well on the plane and insisted on a nap.

Rick suggested to Kevin.

"Let's check out the surroundings where Mary was spotted, for an hour or two."

When they were at the shopping Plaza, where the lead that saw Mary had instructed Philip, Kevin wondered.

"Look at the prices and it's all designer wear. Where the hell does she get the money to shop here in this extravagant place?"

Hardly were his thoughts cold or Rick nudged Kevin. Looking at Rick it was not hard to follow his eyesight. He displayed a shocked expression. A few meters standing away from them, a woman with her back turned to them, stood.

"Crap that looks exactly like her. She's well dressed. Looks well off!" Kevin whispered.

Rick moved speedily forward and dived the woman. When safely on top of her, he held onto her arm, gripping it firmly and pulling it to her back. She turned her head to face Rick and he realized.

"I'm so sorry Mademoiselle, I thought it was a friend of mine, I mean not a friend but someone, who did me in!"

She was the spit image of Mary from the back but when she turned, her facial features were softer and different. It was at that moment that two burly men took Rick by his arms and cuffed him to the nearest pole. They turned to the lady he had assaulted and while helping her to her feet, they asked in shock, if she is all right.

She was crying and saying.

"You're supposed to be my body guards, where the fluff were you, when I needed you? How could you allow such a thing to have happened?"

Stepping forward, Kevin tried to explain.

"Please this is a misunderstanding!" He started.

But the bodyguards ignored him and saw the lady to the limousine and when she was seated comfortably in the back of the limousine holding a glass of something, they un-cuffed Rick and placed him into the following, black Mercedes.

"Where are you taking him?" Kevin asked.

"To police!" They answered rudely in broken English.

"I'll see you at the nearest police station!" Kevin stated to Rick and left.

Needless to say, Kevin waited in vain for two hours for anyone to report the incident and bring Rick in.

Having erred badly, Rick tried apologizing but to no avail and when he realized that his pleas fell on deaf ears, he stayed quiet.

"They cannot do anything worse to me than

having my son killed. I died that day, so I will take what is coming!"

It was in a small building near the right bank of the Seine, where the world's biggest museum displayed itself. The Mercedes parked as close to the Louvre as possible and the two men climbed out, Rick was pulled roughly from the car and forced into the museum and down to the basement. It was on shutting the door, that Rick was interrogated out of reach of all ears and away from the millions of art pieces which filled the museum.

"What is your business here?"

"Were finding Mary Ross!"

"Who is this Mary Ross?"

"Kevin's ex-wife!"

The burly almost fat man, hit Rick across the face, while questioning.

"Why you attack Mademoiselle?"

The fat man now punched him unexpectedly, in the stomach while demanding.

"Speak the truth or we will kill you?"

"I am speaking the truth!" Rick managed to say while trying hard to catch his breath.

"What you want with Mademoiselle?"

"I thought she was Mary Ross!"

"So if she was, why you want her, for what reason?"

"She stole a secret formula from Dr. Ross!"

"What is the formula for?"

Rick stayed quiet now. The two men now made turns to beat Rick until he fell to the floor and they asked again.

"What is the formula for?"

"A serum!" One of the two kicked him in the stomach, shouting.

"Talk!"

"Serum to be injected, making the brain use more of its thinking matter!"

A leg shot out while he lay on the floor and kicked Rick on his upper thigh. The man insisted.

"And if this Serum is injected and makes

one very clever, why has his wife stolen it?"
Rick could hardly get the words out but through the blood running from his mouth, he spluttered.
"She is selling it to different countries for millions of Dollars!"
One suggested.
"I think we should go drop him off where he is staying, but first, what is your name Sir?"
"I'm Rick and staying at the Le Paris!"
The two men did not say a word further, leaving Rick to lie alone and also leaving the building doors, ajar.
Rick tried to get up but could not. He lay there for a long while and eventually started to drag himself with much pain, toward the outside. It was hours later and Rick had neared an intersection of the road. He could hear the sound of cars and tried to stay upright but often fell while waiting for someone to find him. It was an hour later when a car stopped and asked him, if he is okay. The kind man helped him in and took

him right to the hospital. They treated his wounds and he went back to the hotel. The lobby manager looked at him with dismay and called Kevin.

"We have a man asking for you in reception!"

In his heart Kevin knew it was Rick and ran down the stairs, without waiting for the lift.

"Rick, buddy, you did not deserve this!"

And Kevin helped him to the suite.

It was days later when Rick was able to get out of bed and while he still experienced much pain, Kevin could not help reminding him of the incident.

"Were you so convinced that it was Mary?" He asked this while wearing a grin.

"You were even convinced!"

"But to dive her? Ooh. Mademoiselle was angry!"

Having decided by Kevin that Chrystal was to go back home on her own before the men. She was not impressed and played for time.

"Kevin will stay with you, Rick!" She gave a small laugh, and admitted.

"Look at the mess you guys get into, when I'm here, what will it be like when I'm gone?"

"We'll be fine really Chrystal!" Rick soothed.

"By the story that the two of you tell, it sounds to me like two grown men feeling like two boys, in an adventure!" And she rolled her eyes at them.

Diving onto the bed now, Kevin announced.

"Excuse me everyone but I'm going to spend the afternoon right here on this spot with Crystal before she goes back!"

Not stopping from searching his mind, Rick kept saying over and over.

"That looked just like Mary, how could we have confused her so?"

"Not me…you!" Kevin threw back, while breaking into hearty laughter.

His suite was like that of the palace in England, even compared to the luxury of the rest of the building, here in France. It was before having the interview that the client, in broken French, had explained.

"Mary, you are such a beautiful woman. How can any man possess such a divine creature?"

She had giggled while allowing him to hold onto her hand. She felt confident in herself and played the flirting game back.

"And you are what any women would wish to have, as a pillar of strength, by her side!"

He asked.

"Shall we have lunch now, are you ready?"

Mary nodded saying.

"As hungry as can be, thank you!"

He took her hand and led her into the dining room. In the center of the room as big as a hall, stood an antique Barrette dining room suite, set with white, displaying a setting of silver and Chrystal on it. When he pulled her chair out for her, Mary could only think that this way of life was habit forming and she did not mind in the least. The butler standing by, served them and a wine steward stayed a few meters from them, filling up their glasses, when needed.

"I could do with this life!" Mary breathed.

It was after her second glass of wine that Mary felt rather light headed and the charming client had flattered her so, that when he suggested they meet further in the drawing room, she had to focus hard on not slurring. Her mind seemed to be having small blackouts and when she found herself between his sheets, she for the moment could not move, to leave. He was lying at her side, staring at her and when he said.

"I've been watching you sleep and I can see, why many a man would lose his head over you!"

With that he started to kiss her. She could not remember what had in the past while, happened to make her feel this way but succumbed to the ecstasy of the moment. He was charming and a lover like she had not experienced. It was as if he went out of his way only to please her and she thought.

"I think I deserve this!"

Her mind kept reeling, seeing that the deal she was about to close with him, was a done job. She kissed him, making herself more needed and when he breathed in broken French.

Mary knew he was hers and she started to make plans what she was going to do with the money. When he fell back, she bounced from the bed and made for the bathroom. He had risen from the bed when she came back into the room and dressed. While she was brushing her hair, he stood behind her, then holding her even tighter.

Now back in the suite of her client, this room sporting French collections of art and vintage, she knew the same thing had happened, she had become dizzy and had blacked out. It was different now, in the way that she needed to close this 10 Million Dollar deal. She did not want to see him in her life again and it showed on her face.

"I don't know, let us close the deal and see how things go?"

Her statement of wait and see, had immediately set him off to become stand offish and later for Mary, the interview did not at all, go well. She tried to be her charming self but on that alone, she was not able to pull off the deal. In fact, the client had insulted her, with the price offer. He felt since things went wrong for Mary on the island, which he was now going to get a bargain price for the brilliant, stemming with the Jagirremi Serum. Mary was angry.

While sitting in the lounge, Rick teased.

"So you're leaving us, Chrystal?"

She did not answer but turned to Kevin.

"I still don't want to go home without you, Kevin!"

"I insist after today you go back home and be there for the kids and we will carry on here!"

Rick insisted.

"My head aches. I'm going to lie down and give you guys' privacy!"

Chrystal added.

"So go and have a lie down and tomorrow, we will visit the address that Philip gave Kevin. The place where Byron used to have a business and where Mary met him and their affair began!"

Kevin put in now.

"Are you up to it, Rick?"

"As hard as it may be, I'm also wanting answers and the sooner we begin, the better!"

Guilt played in Keven's mind.

"Shall I tell Rick that I killed Byron as he was my wife's lover? How the hell do I do that, after all, I killed his son in cold blood?"

It was also on Chrystal's suggestion that they, Rick, Kevin and Chrystal watch the building where Byron's business was for 24 hours before going in.

"Not many people seem to be using it. No-one has even entered or exited the building besides the Janitor, who seems to stay there!"

Inside the neat building they broke the office lock.

On entering first, Chrystal breathed.

"This is an awesome studio. Look at the paintings and sculptures!" Kevin walked slowly past some of the artefacts and said so all could hear.

"These are very, very good!"

Sounding over wrought now Rick put in.

"Yes, Byron was always the artist one in our family but what he got up to getting involved with Mary, I cannot say, except that was the

beginning of the end!”
Kevin admitted.
“We have at least 20 of his paintings and sculptures in the home. Would never have thought it was he, who did them!”
Chrystal touched lovingly over a painting of nude woman.
“Oh heaven, this is stunning!”

“You know what, were here on official business and the past is now in the past. Let’s get on with the job!”
He was pulling the covers back and exposing more easels, holding paintings, when Kevin in a flat tone, informed.
Rick spoke now.
“Are we going to allow personal feelings to interfere with the case, then we may as well stop right now!”
Rick sat down at the desk and started going through the paperwork. He found a diary with the dates in. Dates of when Mary was going to be in France with Byron. He also

announced.

"Mary's list of prospective clients that she was going to see!"

Chrystal picked up the video and pushed it into the player. Mary appeared, teaching Byron to sell the serum. Teaching him of its ingredients and sales techniques. While standing with his hands on his hips, Kevin stared at the screen. When the clip was finished, he turned his eyes to the floor for a full moment and when he looked up, he announced.

"He was caught in her trap. She over ruled him. He was just a kid!"

Rick added.

"Well, shall we say, we have finished seeing what we needed to see here?"

Chrystal was paging through a file that lay by the cheque book.

"O, O!" She sounded.

"What?" Kevin asked.

"You're the proud owner of this block and everything in it. But hold onto your hats.

You're the proud owner of a helicopter in the buildings helipad!"
Striding to stand next to her, Kevin gasped.
"She bought everything without me knowing, on my name, so no one would suspect her of anything!"
He thought for a moment and when he blurted out.
"I would have been responsible!"
Chrystal and Rick too amplified the same thing.
"But yes, it's all paid!" Chrystal debated, while holding his gaze.
Rick laughed admitting.
"She's coming to kill you, Kevin. She's going to want her "stuff" back!"
"I'll tell you what Rick, I honestly feel I would like to transfer the building into your name. It was your son's studio, after all. It could be good for you!"
Standing up from behind the desk, Chrystal asked in all put on innocence.
"Can I have a comfortable pair of shoes

please, my feet are hurting, Kevin!"
They laughed and Kevin chased her to the door, taking her hand. At the door, each gave their advice input and repaired the catch of the door as best as they could, by using the hair band, belonging to Chrystal.

A full week of hard work went by and Kevin while speaking to Philip on the phone, disclosed.
"Nowhere. She is nowhere to be seen. We have found a small lead going to check it out tomorrow. It does not look promising after the week of enquiring to her whereabouts and showing her photo around!" He stopped and added.
"And Chrystal playing it day for day when I said she must get to the kids and she does not want to budge!"
Philip laughed saying.
"That's my Sis. The kids are all content, stop worrying. Come back, let us wait our time till we have something more!"

"Actually it breaks my heart to say this but this was a cul de sac. The only one who achieved any good from it was Rick!"

Rick who had been sitting on the sofa reading, now gave an enquiring look. Kevin announced into the receiver.

"Yes, he scored a room full of beautifully done paintings, I'd say that in itself should be worth a pretty penny!"

On that same evening, while they were seated in the lounge, Rick started to say.

"I did everything for that boy, I put everything into raising him as one expects to. He was my pride and joy. Was it her beauty or her charm or was it the lack in something that I did not teach him that caused him to fall for her, a married women!"

"Let me stop you right there Rick. She was charming and knew how to work with men. Do you think I was the only man in her life, do you think us, Byron and me, and were the only men in her life?" Kevin waited but went on to say.

"No, she could not be satisfied with one man, ever!" He carried on though.

"I'd say you must not blame yourself for anything. If I can make out what is going on here, is that Mary offered Byron a pretty fair amount to do the job, he did!"

"I don't know how to get over his death. I don't know how to be without my best friend. I don't know who I am or what life is about, without my son any more. He told me, Dad you will never lack anything in your life again and I want you to go with me, where I can make sure that you are safe. Life just is not the same anymore!"

Guilt ate at Kevin's being but he knew he could not tell Rick that he was the one who killed his son. Kevin cared too much for Rick, to be that honest and he kept his secret well hidden, even from Chrystal.

The following day, Kevin instructed Chrystal.

"Seeing you played me, day for day, to stay

another day, if you want you can do the packing and Rick and I will check out for a new lead and we'll see you later!"
It was in the foyer of a hotel, a man had looked at Mary's photo and advised.
"Oh yes, I see the lady, she shops very often at the market!"
Kevin had added.
"Yes, she does love shopping!"
"I see her at the stalls with the scarves often!" The man advised.
Excited now that they had a definite lead, neither Kevin nor Rick could wait for the following day to investigate this but immediately headed for the market. It was neither Rick nor Kevin that saw the black Mercedes C-class, following them. The car moved slowly alongside them, until it parked and two men climbed out. The men disappeared between the Plaza stores, while every now and then appearing only to make sure of the where about of Kevin and Rick. Rick and Kevin were positive that they

were onto the right track, oblivious of men who not only knew Mary and her business, but also knew the fact that Kevin was the top surgeon that had discovered the Jagirremi Serum. This serum, they knew that Mary so freely, among those with money, advertised, could be a good investment. If Kevin for one moment stopped to think of his own safety, his well-being, he, Kevin, had only one matter in mind and that was to find Emma.

It was when Kevin at the scarves stall, searched with his eyes as women of all shapes and sizes made their way shopping, searching through the millions of scarves, when suddenly Kevin felt the hard steel metal of a pistol press in between his ribs and a voice quietly said.

"Move to the right and get into the Black Mercedes at the side of the road. Kevin looked for Rick and noticed him on the far side with his back facing, still searching earnestly for Mary. Kevin tried to ease his body from the pressure against the pistol but it was only pushed harder into his back, forcing him to quickly get into the black Mercedes.

On turning, Rick immediately saw that Kevin was not standing on the spot where he was last seen but to his dismay, he watched Kevin being forced at gunpoint, into the black Mercedes. Rick quickly made for the first yellow cab and pushed away the man trying to get in, apologizing.

"I'm sorry, I have an emergency, and my wife is having a baby!" And Rick jumped in, shutting the cab door, while saying.

"Cabbie, see that black Mercedes on the other side. Follow him but don't allow him to see us!"

The cab driver immediately sat upright, stared for a moment at the Mercedes before he pulled away at some speed. It was when being sure of following the right car and keeping to a moderate speed that the Cabbie first spoke. He did not take his eyes from his driving and stayed hidden behind another car in another lane, to the Mercedes, before the driver looked in the mirror. His eyes met those of Rick and he said in broken English, while wearing a satisfied smile.

"Twenty years, I've been doing this job. For twenty years, I practiced every day for this day. Every day, I waited to hear my passenger say.

"Follow that car!"

And today it happened!"

His eyes were glued to the Mercedes and when it stopped, Rick ordered.

"Quick stop, right here!"

When the Mercedes pulled into a driveway, Rick drew his wallet out without taking his eyes from the driveway. He placed a 20 Dollar note down and jump from the car. He walked over the road to where the driveway was, waited a while and then entered. Darkness was falling and he was trying as much as possible to hide in shadows. When he heard voices, he went closer to the house and through the lit up windows, he could see Kevin fastened to a chair, in the study. He was being interrogated.

"Are you Dr. Kevin Ross and are you the one, who came up with the formula of the Jagirremi Serum?

"Where is the formula, Kevin?"

"It has been stolen by Mary. If you can find Mary, she has the formula!"

"What is your business here?"

Kevin stayed quiet and then the taller of the two men, took a horse whip from the desk and beat Kevin, while demanding, over and over.

"Talk or we will make you talk!"

The blows had reigned over his shoulders and body and when the man hit him with full force by using his fist, Kevin folded, stating.

"To find Mary, she has my daughter!"

The two men looked at each other.

"Your daughter is the pregnant one, yes?"

Kevin kept his mouth shut now.

"I'm not a mind reader but these men are getting ideas!" He declared to himself only.

The man with the horse whip brought down the whip on Kevin's chest and he answered in a soft tone.

"Yes!"

While having reached the passage now, Rick looked around for a place to hide. As the sound from his movement was absorbed by the luxury carpets, he chose to enter the room closest to the study where Kevin was and crawled in behind the sofa, where he lay for a long while.

Rick listened as the men, questioned Kevin and when they left the room, he waited for all sound to become still.

By this time Chrystal had packed and gone to supper on her own and neither Kevin nor Rick had made their appearance. She was worried but knew that they would look out for each other.

The two men had decided to leave Kevin tied up, while they thought of a plan to rather, get Emma into their hands. They left the room and in a television room, while smoking, discussed their plans further away from the ears of Kevin. It was when they were settled in the T.V Room that Rick heard one of them make a call. When they addressed the person on the phone, telling. "Mademoiselle, we have hit the jackpot here!" And then he started to speak French further. It was then when Rick snuck into the study and when Kevin looked up into his eyes, Rick almost burst out laughing to see his relief. Rick showed him to be quiet and from the desk took the mail opener and released the rope that was tied at Kevin's ankles and wrists.

"You look a mess Buddy!" He whispered to Kevin.

Quietly they left again, going out through the door that was still standing open and into the night. It was when going through the front gate that a car without its lights on, at a speed stopped right next to them.

Kevin spat saying.

"Oh Shit, they have both of us now!"

Laughing with great relief sounding, Rick assured it's the cab!"

The cabby spoke.

"Excuse me Sir, but you paid me enough for the last ride to wait, so here I am!"

Breaking out into soft painful laughter, Kevin followed the story behind, this happening. Kevin cringed when he tried to laugh, his lips were broken and it felt as if his body was on fire from the lashings. For both Kevin and Rick it was a relief to be in the cab, making their way back to Chrystal and safety. Rick could not thank the driver enough and gave him another 20 Dollars.

"Well you deserve to be flat broke!" Was all Chrystal had to say to them, adding.

"You were supposed to stay together, what were you thinking?"

No one left to go back to the Island as

Kevin needed recuperating from broken ribs and facial injuries. Kevin stayed in bed and Chrystal decided.

"Rick seeing you feel up to it, just so we don't lose time, I will accompany you and we'll search the stores for Mary!"

Chrystal wore a scarf and sunglasses. Mary would not have easily recognized her. She stood at the scarves and accessories store and allowed her eyes to search. It was by late morning, when she spotted Mary accompanied by Emma. Mary did not look as if her mood was good and Chrystal stood back behind the wall, so as not to be seen. Her heart was pounding now, she followed them from store to store. Rick seemed to have lost time because he disappeared from Chrystal's sight and she found herself, too afraid to find him first and to take her eyes from Emma and Mary. Later Chrystal followed Emma and Mary back to their hotel.

"It's the same hotel as we are in!" Chrystal

exclaimed.

 Satisfied now to know exactly where they were staying, she left to their suite. When running into Rick before she could give him hell, he gave her a scolding.

"I have been searching for you for over an hour!"

"And I, dear Sir, have been following Mary and Emma to their hotel from the Plaza!"

He gave a surprised look, asking.

"You know where they stay?"

She nodded with a smile.

"I'll take you there in the morning!" She teased not saying the hotel's name.

It was as if Chrystal had a confidence boost because she now scolded Rick, saying.

"No wonder you and Kevin missed each other and no wonder Kevin and you got beaten up!"

"What are we doing wrong in your eyes?" Kevin asked while still in much pain.

"I stood searching for Mary for over an hour and I happened not to miss them, but what of my cover, where was Rick? Anything could have happened to me, like it happened to you Kevin and you Rick!”

With her finger, she now prodded Kevin in the ribs, he cringed and she put her hands to her mouth.

“I’m so sorry, Darling!”

He in turn straightened and said.

“I had you fooled, I’m feeling better and will accompany you to look out and follow Mary tomorrow!”

“Are you sure you’ll be up to it. Why don’t you take another day and stay in bed!”

After she had kissed him he explained.

“I’m not allowing you to enter the danger zone by yourself. In any case, I want to kill that bitch with my bare hands, myself!”

Rick asked out of the blue.

“Are you sure it was not the bloody woman that Kevin and I mistook for Mary. She looked much like her!”

“No, it is Mary. I talked to her for long enough, Rick!”

"In any case Emma was with her, pregnant Emma!"

"Shall we be at the hotel entrance at sunrise, so we don't miss her?"

"Definitely!" They agreed.

It was the crack of dawn, when Chrystal let them to the opposite corner of the hotel and said.

"She's in the same hotel. Don't let her see you!"

Kevin and Rick waited, each standing at the opposite corner and she, Chrystal while wearing her scarf and sunglasses waited near the hotel exit. It was much later after midday and Mary had not shown. Chrystal walked over to where Kevin was standing, He looked pale.

"What's wrong?"

"Going through hell with the painful ribs!"

"I'm going in!" Chrystal announced pertly, adding.

I have had enough of this waiting in any

case I'm well-disguised!"

While her eyes scoured the very large foyer, Chrystal made for the reception desk. "Excuse me, what room Mary Ross?" She asked in broken language.

The reception clerk stared at the woman before him, he was sure he knew her but she was wearing sunglasses and a scarf and he explained.

"Mrs. Ross, she left early this morning, probably five o'clock!" He said this, while wearing a big smile.

Not believing their luck, Chrystal asked.

"Are you sure, could you check the book please, she was here yesterday!"

Chrystal did carry on to ask, though.

"Did she leave a forwarding address?"

"Yes in fact, she did say that she is on her way to Greece!"

He bent his head over the book and again assured her, while still beaming, that Mary had booked out.

When Chrystal found herself outside at the

hotel entrance and into the street, she noticed Kevin and Rick, still together.

"She booked out probably just before we got here!"

"The bitch!" Kevin breathed, also saying.

"I went through hell today for her, actually for the satisfaction of killing her!"

Chrystal laughed into her hand, breathing.

"You're so full of aches and pains, doubt if you could kill a fly!"

He threw her a "not appreciated" look. They were all disappointed and went back to their suit, after Crystal had removed the scarf and sunglasses. In anger Keven acknowledged.

"I don't know how the hell, she keeps slipping through our fingers!"

The phone rang early evening and Chrystal answered.

"Hi, Sis can I speak to one of the guys, just want to know if they are any the wiser?"

"You can in a minute. Brace yourself, I saw

Mary and Emma and followed them back to their hotel. Guess what the name is? The Sbibvon Chateau!"

"Some detective you have here, that's where you are staying!"

She laughed while throwing a glance at Rick but carried on to say.

"Yes, he was off course standing in a trance, not even noticing, that I had taken the car. When I got to the reception desk, the officer assured me that they had booked out, earlier!"

Philip now in turn, debated in certainty, with her.

"No, they fooled you!"

"Really, the guy at the desk told me she left a forwarding address for Greece!"

"Fooled you!" Philip teased.

"Well, then I don't know what to say!"

"Don't believe anything anyone tells you, besides me off course!"

"Well I am going there tomorrow and I'll give the reception clerk hell for lying to me!"

Chrystal acknowledged.

Philip added before greeting.

"Don't waste your breath!"

Chrystal walked back into the lounge and shared this news with Kevin and Rick.

In the hotel Sbibvon Chateau, the reception clerk did not recognize Chrystal but realized that, while wearing a scarf and dark glasses, might be one of the persons, they at the hotel have been warned against, keeping a watch for and reporting anything out of the ordinary, as the owner, who was involved with the illegal transactions. But with his interest in getting the formula, he was clever and had prepared his people.

"I cannot afford to get into trouble with the law, there is too much at stake here and this deal is big, huge!"

When the reception clerk had set off the alarm, it soundlessly warned the owner of trouble and while the owner watched what was happening on the screen, he had ordered.

"Get rid of anyone that asks for them again. Well done!"

In their suite Chrystal threw the phone down from speaking to Philip and said.

"She left late this afternoon after we had been there and if anyone says I was fooled, I'll strangle them with my bare hands!"

"Shit we missed her again!"

Kevin reiterated.

"I missed my Emma again?"

"Kevin we will find her, I just know we'll get her back!"

Chrystal put in now, advising.

"Tell me when you guys are strong enough to leave. I've had Mary in chunks!"

Travelling back on the plane, Kevin was quiet, he was worrying about Emma being involved with this scheme of Mary. He turned to Chrystal complaining.

"What lasting effect will this instability have on her and worse still on the baby. Emma should be home with us, where she knows, she is safe and so is my grandchild!"

"I assure you once Emma is in the security back home, with her dad at her side and with her family, she will be fine. As for the little one, we will give him so much love, he won't have time to feel insecure. Now I want you to relax. We will find her. Every lead we get we will follow, till Emma is home!"

She kissed him while on the plane and stroked his cheek.

The plane lifted and bumped slightly while Kevin was saying.

"Strange how you know what to say to make me feel better. One would think you are a psychiatrist!"

She laughed answering him.

"Maybe, I'm a very good psychiatrist!"

She thought for a moment and added.

"Maybe I just love my husband to be, very much and will do anything to help him feel better!"

The sound of the intercom came on and the

Captain announced.

"Were experiencing much turbulence due to a bad storm. Please all fasten your seat belts!"

Chrystal drew the curtains to close out the lightening which lit up the night skies.

"I feel uneasy about this storm!"

"I'm sure it'll blow over soon!" Kevin soothed.

With all the curtains on the plane now drawn, it seemed as if the turbulence was more concentrated on and Kevin was sitting upright, as if tense but he tried not showing it.

"Don't want Chrystal to worry!"

She was quiet. Rick who had been sleeping in the seat next to her, was awake now.

"What's happening?" He asked.

"Turbulence!" Chrystal filled him in.

"Okay!" He soothed with false placidness.

The plane lifted once again and the pilot's voice, sounded.

"Ladies and Gentleman, we apologize for

the inconvenience but were having engine problems and want to assure you, we are doing everything we can, to overcome this problem!"

No one spoke. Eventually Rick changed places with Kevin, in order for Kevin to be sitting next to her. She took Kevin's hand in hers and said.

"I'm afraid!"

"Don't be. We're together aren't we?"

She nodded and looked away when the plane hit a pocket. She started crying softly and put her head against Kevin's shoulder. He put out his hand placing it around her, holding her to him, he whispered.

"I love you, always have and always will!"

"I love you too!" She cried between tears.

The Captains voice sounded.

"Ladies and Gentleman we are turning back to France and again just want to apologize for the inconvenience!"

Chrystal was the first to speak and in a whisper, disclosed to Kevin.

"I hope we make it!"

That was at the moment that the Captain spoke again.

"Ladies and Gentlemen, we have too much fuel to make a safe landing, so we are going to empty the fuel tanks over the ocean. Please believe, we are in control and are doing the best that we can, for you!"

There was tension in the plane and no one said anything. They could feel as the fuel left the tanks and Chrystal asked, without expecting an answer.

"And if they let out, too much?"

As her husband to be Kevin stood his place full, in trying to make her feel safe and he explained.

"They are familiar with what amount they would need to take us back to De Gaulle Airport. Now stop worrying. Were together aren't we?"

In Rick's mind many things played out

before him. He saw Byron before him. He spoke to him.

"My Son, I have missed you and now our plane is in trouble. It does not worry me as I have lay awake night after night, wondering where you are, did you die with much pain, where do we go. I've wondered when it is my time if you will be the one appointed to fetch me home."

He wiped at the tears that threatened to fall, before carrying on.

"Son, I died already when you were taken, nothing can be worse. I'm ready to go and wait on you, if you are to guide me through. I am at peace!"

Kevin loosed his seat belt to turn and hold Chrystal. Her shoulders shook with sobs that were smothered by a handful of tissues. Kevin kissed her head over and over, saying.

"It's going to be okay, you know I'm not too good with my fists but my head tells me, we are going to be okay!"

Rick leaned over and placed his hand on Kevin's shoulder.

"Thanks Buddy, thanks for everything, you meant to me!"

And then reaching for Chrystal's hand, Rick said.

"We're going to be okay, Chrystal!"

She wiped at her eyes, while she spoke.

"Thanks Rick, just very emotional. Waited for many years for the man, I had lost once before!"

The plane hit another air pocket and straightened out. The Captains voice sounded again. Chrystal remembered thinking that he sounded tense and informed Kevin so.

"Ladies and Gentlemen, were getting ready to make an emergency landing, will you wear the oxygen masks, fasten your seat belts and place your heads onto your laps, please?"

Kevin kissed Chrystal and Rick shook Kevin's hand. When lying on their laps each played with his own thoughts.

Her head was so full of questions, as she asked.

"I've just got the love of my life back, how can this be?"

Kevin on the other hand was thankful that he and Chrystal were together again but wondered what will become of his daughter and her baby, when he was not there, trying to find her.

In turn Rick was lying with his hands folded and lying on his arms quietly. Sobs were heard from the inside of the plane and soothing voices sounded.

The plane was going slowly into the landing. When Kevin stared out of the window, ambulance lights were flashing all over, near the runway and on touch down, the pilot braked and the plane hit the runway just to lift again and bounced at a speed down the runway. The sound of ambulances came, when they came to a very bumpy stop. The Captain reminded.

"Ladies and Gentlemen when the doors open, please give the shute a moment to open before sliding as fast as you can down and moving as far from the plane as possible, in case of fire or explosion. Thank you Ladies and Gentlemen!"
Chrystal lifted the oxygen mask and said aloud.
"Geez that sounded final!"

At the door, Kevin and Rick assisted Chrystal down onto the Shute before they in turn expelled themselves down. Ambulances sounded their alarms and were assisting people and taking them speedily to the airport entrance to safety. The fire brigade moved in.

The airport was taking them back to the hotel where the passengers last stayed, till further arrangements will be made. That night in the luxury suite, Chrystal lay quietly eating through another "Welcome to the Hotel Sbibvon Chateau, bouquet of chocolates", thankful that the ordeal was over.

It was the following day that Kevin suggested they do some shopping. While Chrystal was busy in a store and Rick was waiting at a restaurant, Kevin looked up and saw Emma, but Mary was at her side. He knew under no circumstances was she supposed to even suspect that he was close, or she would take Emma and flee once again. He had his cellphone with him and immediately phoned Philip.

"I'm following Mary and Emma!"

Silent for a moment only, Philip ordered.

"Get away there, you are endangering the baby and Emma!"

Pressing something on the phone Kevin closed it and pushed it into his pocket.

"My daughter, no ways, I want my daughter!"

He followed them further as they shopped and by evening, he was surprised to see that they disappeared into the same hotel where they were supposed to have moved from. He watched from far to see where the lift stopped and then went to his suite. When he walked in Chrystal asked.

"Where were you?"

"Following Mary and Emma!"

Her mouth hung open and she exclaimed.

"Are they still here, are you sure they not in Greece?"

"Slowly now, one question at a time. They never left. They still up on the top landing suite!"

"Well I never!"

Turning to Rick now, Kevin stated.

"Were going to get into that suite somehow and I'm taking Emma. To hell with Mary. Someone else can get her!"

It was hardly midnight when Kevin and Rick took the lift to e top floor of the building.

"Geez, it's beautiful up here. Look at the paintings. Can you imagine what they cost?"

Rick showed with his finger to his lips. Kevin tried the door, allowing the knob to turn and he wiggled it trying gently, to force it open. Rick had tried another door and it was open. Kevin made a dash to the room and Rick showed him again with a finger at his lips to be quiet. Inside the room were two empty beds. Kevin threw Rick a glance. By the bedside there were pairs of shoes and on the bed lay jewelry that young girls wear. He exclaimed.

"It's Emma's!"

"Are you sure?"

"Definitely!"

"What do you want us to do?"

"We'll come back!" But he added.

"Let us look around if we can get in?"

Rick felt the adjoining door handle and it too was open. Kevin amplified.

"It's Mary's room!"

"Sure?"

"I smell her perfume!"

"Shall we look for the briefcase?"

Kevin grinned at the request Rick had just made and allowed his eyes to search the room. Voices sounded and Rick whispered.

"Were going to be caught here. Quick under the bed!"

In the darkness, Kevin lay as if already dead. He whispered to Rick.

"Oh Shit, I have to pull my legs in and hold them bent slightly, my knee!"

Rick showed a finger to his lips when the voices neared. Mary opened the adjoining door while she was talking to Emma.

"It's been a helluva unsuccessful day and I'm clapped!"

Neither Rick nor Kevin dared move now but when they heard her getting into the bath, they made for the door, leading to the passage.

Chrystal waited up for them and the following day it was when Security was going through the film of the hotel of the previous evening, that they came upon the piece where Rick and Kevin, were snooping around Mary's room. The owner of the hotel was now afraid of his reputation as he'd been doing underhanded deals and immediately sent for Mary to come to the Security room and see the footage.

"It's Kevin!" She exclaimed!
And they Emma and Mary, were speedily assisted into leaving the hotel. When Mary had ordered Emma to pack, she was excited as it was to be back to the arms of her man.
Not feeling ashamed at holding up everyone!"

Mary tried to sound pleasant when she contacted Gavin, to say that she was on her way back. He could hear by her voice tone that things did not go well.

"I'm glad you're coming home, I'll be there to meet you!"
When Gavin fetched her, he allowed her to cry, while he held her. He did not ask

questions. Gavin knew the less you know where it concerns Mary, the better for one.

Being back in the Swiss Alps for Emma was divine but she really expected her mother somehow, to have made contact with her Dad. And when alone and sitting in the crook of Anton's arms, Emma told him of her father.
"He is a great dad, and you're going to love him!"

For Rick, Kevin and Chrystal when they did find out for themselves, that Mary and Emma fled, it was a disappointment and they too left for home on the island.

6 THE ISLAND

They had been back on the island for exactly ten days before Chrystal pointed out to Kevin.

"You know that you make no secret of being edgy!"

"I'm not edgy, I might rather be needy, needing more attention from you!" He said, while wearing a grin.

"Kevin Ross, I give you every bit of me, what more could I do?"

"I'll tell you what, let me from my side, and do something for you for a change!"

This sent Chrystal into laughter, amplifying.

"You cannot even boil an egg, what have you in mind?"

"My secret, Mrs. Ross, to be!"

"We haven't even got engaged yet and not to talk about the divorce!"

Kevin was immediately on the defense.

"I don't even consider myself married to her anymore and James is busy with the divorce, she owes me big time. Nothing stops us from getting engaged, so I know too, that you have made a promise to marry me and you cannot get out of it or I can sue you!"

This statement sent them both into fits of laughter. It was just then that David walked in, asking.

"What's up with you, guys?"

Kevin stole a glance at Chrystal, before he started.

"Well you know Mom and I are being divorced?"

"Old news and now about time, is Uncle James not taking rather long about things?"

"Uncle James is doing his job, it's your Mom that is flitting all over and he is waiting for her to be where he can get hold of her!"

"Well Dad, what Mom has done, I'm ashamed to say, she deserves to be locked up and I think that is where uncle James is going to find her, eventually! He will"

Being David's mother that was being discussed, Chrystal did not say a word, she did feel sorry for him, though. Through the months that she had talked to the children, she grew to love them, feeling sorry that Mary had done such a deed.

Searching for words now, Kevin said to David.

"I was just saying to Chrystal that it would be nice for me to belong and have someone at my side, helping me too!"

David laughed at Kevin and explained.

"Dad you and Chrystal are in love, don't make excuses now. I would love to have Chrystal by your side, too. I mean, after some of the not so nice women, I've seen that have tried to charm you and I would hate it if one of them, were to be my step mom!"

Giving Kevin a slap on the shoulder now, Chrystal was laughing aloud, saying.

"Which women David, if you go with me, we can go sort them out!"

Half embarrassed now, Kevin started.

"Well son, would you mind if I asked Chrystal for her hand in marriage!"

Acting sternly now, David gave his view of the matter.

"Dad, I insist that she make an honest man of you, by marriage!"

Laughter broke out now, filling the room.

David carried on to say.

"I give thee, Kevin permission to take Chrystal as my step mom. And Chrystal thank you, for everything you mean to us!"

Hugging him now, Chrystal wiped her eyes, she had started crying but spoke through her tears.

"Thank you David for accepting me. You too have made my dream of having children come true!"

Turning now to face Kevin, David asked.

"Dad, how about you asking Chrystal, now!"

He pretended not to catch what David was saying and asked.

"Ask her what, Son?"

"To marry you, Dad?"

"Oh that, I will still ask her, Son!"

"It is okay Dad you can ask her in my presence, I want to be a part of it!"

Keven disappeared to the room. When he came back to the living room, he walked over to stand in front of Chrystal and when he opened his mouth to speak, David stopped him.

"Not like that, Dad. Down on one knee!"

Chrystal was standing holding her hands before her mouth, she was laughing and crying at the same time.

Kevin went down on one knee and looked up to her.

"Would you marry me, Chrystal?" He asked.

David added.

"Dad what about saying, why you want to marry her?"

While staring at him, Kevin turned to Crystal and stated.

"Because I love you Chrystal!"

He was still perched on one knee while looking from David to Chrystal when she had already stopped crying but started laughing heartily when he asked if he could change knees as.

"This leg is hurting badly, by the amount of time I'm perched here waiting for you to give your answer!"

David turned to her and asked.

"Do you Chrystal say yes, to the proposal from Kevin, on behalf of David and I speak for my sister Emma, too?"

"Chrystal stopped laughing and said.

"Yes definitely David!"

"And me?" Kevin asked pretending to be disappointed.

She bent down and kissed him softly and soothed.

"Yes, more than anything I have ever wanted in my life, I will marry you!"

David now asked.

"So when?"

Kevin was staring at him.

"When will you marry her dad?"

"David, as soon as James ties up the divorce!"

David replied.

"Oh! Is that okay for you, Chrystal?"

"Thank you spokesman, David that will be in order!"

Clearing his throat now, Kevin reminded.

"I'm still busy standing on my painful knee, here!"

Breaking out into laughter Chrystal again leaned down and kissed him. Kevin took her hand and placed a diamond engagement ring onto her finger.

Through her tears she was staring at the ring, breathing.

"Oh Kevin it is so beautiful!"

He in desperate tone, asked.

"Am I allowed to get up now, please?"

He was roaring with laughter when David put out his hand and said at the same time he was pulling his father into a standing position. Then David shook his hand, stating.

"For the record, let me be the first to congratulate you, Dad!"

Kevin pulled him close and hugged him.

"Thanks Son!"

David then turned to Chrystal and said.

"Welcome to the family, Aunty Chrystal!"

And gave her a warm hug.

It was late evening, David was away spending the evening with Magda and Philip. Speaking to Chrystal now, Kevin asked.

"Do you remember, I promised you an evening with a surprise and you said, I cannot even boil an egg?"

Chrystal met Kevin's gaze, she wondered what he had in mind but left asking, so it could be a surprise!”

She smiled when he disappeared to the bathroom thinking he was going to shower. Chrystal spent the afternoon in the garden and was lounging on the bed, paging through a magazine, before she wanted to take a shower. She fell asleep. When Kevin woke her and stood before her, reaching out his hands for hers, she said.

“Shoo. That must have been some day, I’m clapped. I’m sure it’s the sun!”

He pulled her up, kissed her and started to loosen the loose shirt she had worn, for her day of gardening. He loosed her skinny jeans, pushing him to fall back onto the bed and then while taking each foot by turn into his hand, pulled at the legs of the jeans saying.

“Geez, how do you get these off?” He laughed while he said this but fitted his fingers into the leg pipes and started pulling the jeans down. It was a sight to behold. Crystal screeched with laughter.

“Kevin you’re quite useless at removing a women’s clothing off!” “Well, the darn things seem to suck on to you!"

He pulled his to a standing position, kissed her, saying as he wrapped a big white towel around her and pulled her to the bathroom.

"It's to your benefit that I am useless removing women's clothing!"

On walking into the bathroom she breathed.

"Oh, Kevin you remembered, I love bathing in lavender salts. Where on earth did you find some, on the island?"

"I told you I'm going to spoil you!"

He dropped a few drops of lavender oil into the small lamp and when he saw that she was settled in the bath with a small rolled towel behind her head, he put some soothing music on and left the room. He returned within minutes and brought her a glass of white wine and then while perching himself on the loo seat cover, stayed comfortably for as long as she spoke.

"Oh gosh, this is just what the doctor ordered!" She took a sip of wine and lay back. Kevin left the room.

It was when she appeared from the

bathroom after thirty relaxing minutes, that she noticed the massage bed, inside the room.

"Are you going to massage me, Kevin?" She giggled.

He did not answer and she carried on to say.

"Or am I now supposed to have the energy to massage you?"

He smiled and told her to lie down and he closed her with a warm towel.

"Enjoy!" He said and left again.

The door opened immediately and a lady masseuse came in carrying the necessary warm towels and oils.

"Hi Chrystal, I am Louise and will be doing your massage!"

Chrystal tensed up slightly and whispered.

"Never had this before, what must I do?"

"You will just relax and I will remove every bit of tension from you, well that is what is left after that lovely smelling bath, you just had!"

To Chrystal this was a treat she had never allowed herself, in all the years of hard work, she had been through.

"Your husband tells me you are a pillar to many, through their bad times and I can feel in your shoulders and back muscles, how much strain you have been taking. Now you can just lie back and enjoy the massage!"

And she did lie back and enjoy and Chrystal for that evening, said to Kevin.

"I'm useless even in bed now. After that bath and that massage, really I'm bushed!"

"You should be. A massage like that cleanses and tones every sensory nerve in your body. It is as if you have been detoxed for days. Let's go to bed!"

By the time Kevin had tidied, Chrystal was fast asleep.

He laughed softly and kissed her on the cheek.

"No response!"

He crawled into bed, put his arms around her and with a smile playing at his mouth, he too fell asleep. Having gone to bed early, Chrystal was rested by the crack of dawn. She opened her eyes to feel Kevin's arms still tightly around her and Chrystal wiggled her butt into him, waking him. He snuggled into her saying.

"What a brilliant morning, waking with you!"

"You owe me something!" She declared.

"And what may that be?"

"You never made love to me last night!"

"You were asleep when I came to bed!"

"Well do it now. Before the ring was on my finger it was not your duty but now it is!" She demanded and broke out giggling.

He stretched lazily while first giving a yawn and then he leaned over and with pouted lips, lay waiting for her to kiss him. Chrystal laughed.

"You're so funny, Kevin!"

She stared at his pouted lips and said.

"When we were in the back of the Austin, you did not pout like that!"

"Show me what I did differently!"

"Well for starters, you did not close your eyes, as if you needed to be blind to what you were doing!"

She was still lying perched on her elbow. He had opened his eyes and was laughing.

"Okay show me with the lips, what I used to do!"

She jumped up and sat on top of him and started to kiss him.

He exclaimed.

"That hard, did I kiss you that hard?"

"No, but I want you to feel passion!"

And she lowered her lips and kissed him gently.

"Ahh, that's better!" He commented.

"No running commentary here, please and thank you!"

She slipped down kissing him from his ears into his neck and down to his navel where she stopped, pulled a face and said.

"I'll leave that part to you after you have had a wax!"

He was laughing aloud now and he took her wrists and threw her down onto the bed and said.

"This is how I did it!"

She held her eyes closed and in her mind she was again, at his touch in the back of the Austin. When at last he fell back, he stated.

"And that is how I do it and did it to you. Can you remember it?"

"Gosh I can't utter a word, leave me to lay

here until life ebbs back into me!”

They slumbered for a while and when she felt Kevin stirring to get up, she insisted.

“Mmm. Yummy for bacon and eggs!”

“I thought you said I can’t boil an egg!” He asked.

He stared at her with a smile and said.

“Only because I’m in love with you, I could have it here in half hour!”

“Mmm. She breathed.

“Sounds like my type of man!”

It was later in the morning when David arrived home. Chrystal as always was pottering in the garden and when David saw Kevin sitting in the Gazebo, reading his newspaper, he asked.

“Dad what about a day of surfing?”

Chrystal looked up from what she was doing and said.

“Yes, let’s!”

Surprised by her reaction, Kevin, while still holding the newspaper in the air, asked Chrystal.

“Is that what you really want to do? You

know David and I are experienced surfers!”

“Yes that is what I really want to do, some tanning while you guys catch up!”

Staring at David now, Kevin did not utter a word.

“Yes Dad, let’s go, please!”

It was Chrystal that spoke first, saying.

“I’m going to get ready!”

The two men were already waiting quite a while, before Chrystal arrived, carrying a basket with eats. They left immediately while Kevin carried the basket and his surf board.

It was a perfect day to be out and in the distance, a whale was thrashing around its tail, for all to see. A few holiday makers were sitting around picnic baskets and some of the Muni-landers were walking. Chrystal seemed to know everyone on the Island and stopped every now and again to chat and introduce her family.

When they reached the spot where Kevin and David had last surfed, the two men disappeared into the water. Chrystal shook her head breathing.

“Men, they’re just like children!” And she

turned onto her towel and rubbed oil over her body. The sun was warm and she fell into an almost trance, dozing and waking but when Kevin arrived back from the water and lay down over her, while wearing his wet suit, Chrystal wiggling herself out under him. David was roaring with laughter but reached out his hand to help Chrystal up. She placed the basket within their reach and they sat down to a hearty meal, chatting all the while, until the two men left to surf.

From the distance of the waves at the deeper part of the ocean, Kevin threw a glance to see if Chrystal was okay.

"Dad you know Chrystal will be fine."

"There's a guy just hanging around, I don't like it!"

"You're being jealous, Dad. Yes, Chrystal has everything that a guy wants!"

Kevin glared at his son but David spoke on.

"She's waited for you since the two of you, were students. What more can you want. If you're not happy with that dad we'll have to get a dog because you won't find more faithful than that!"

Scooping water with his hands while perched on the surf board, Kevin sent sheets of water to rain down on his son. David was laughing and when the lift of a wave took him, he was not ready and it rolled him. Spitting and coughing now, David landed at the water's edge. Chrystal had seen him and ran to where the sea spat him out. She asked.
"Are you okay?"
"He nodded!"
"Just feel a fool!" He grinned.
"Where's your father?" Chrystal asked.
On the horizon a small motorboat, disappeared.

In the boat, were three men, one being Kevin. Driving the boat, was a very well built man with a bald head and the other was the one who had pulled Kevin beneath the water, until the boat had stopped, and they had pulled Kevin on board. The bald headed man spoke loudly portraying a French accent.

"Were taking you to the work island and there we want you to give us the formula!"

"I don't have the formula, my ex-wife stole

the hard drive!”

“Well, we have time, seeing it is weekend, so for you to go through your notes and find the formula, we will wait!”

“I don’t understand what the hell you want with me?”

“We tied you to the chair in France you remember, you escaped. We followed you from France, your wife told us of your brilliance and we turned down her offer to buy the child and the formula for 10 Million. She’s a shark, now we fetch the original formula without the added mercury, right from the source and we get it for nothing. Yes. And we kill you for nothing and no one is the wiser!”

Another added.

“They will think you were snorkeling or something when they find the body!”

Perspiring now, Kevin was still in his wetsuit and he stared at the ocean, thinking.

“No way out to making a getaway, just water everywhere, I’ll have to go with them!”

He also soothed to himself.

“Never been good with my fists but my brain can handle much!”

It was on the work Island that Kevin tried to stay calm. There was not a soul around, it being weekend. At the building, Kevin opened the electronic door with his watch and at the lift, the men shouted at him.

"Get us to where the formula is?"

Not knowing what his next move could be, Kevin pressed 5, the doors closed immediately and at 5, the lift stopped with a slight bump. Searching on the laptop for any notes to the formula, Kevin was seated with his head down. The two men looked around and spoke to each other, in French.

Kevin breathed.

"Ah, here is something!"

This caught the attention of both men, who immediately made their way toward him.

He informed.

"I'll just print it out for you!"

They looked pleased. The humming sound of the printer started and they both made their way toward the machine, receiving the bargain they thought they had, for the day. It was in a split second that Kevin made for the lab door. Before they could think to chase him, he was already running up the stairs to the Helipad. They in turn drew out pistols and followed the sound of the footsteps, up. Kevin ran to the edge of the roof and leaned over, his heart was pounding, and he jumped trying as hard as possible to make a soundless landing on the balcony of the lab.

"If she could do it, who am I not to!"

When he dropped to the stone floor, he glanced up at the roof and made his way back up the stairs, to the upper landing door leading out, onto the helipad and by pressing his watch, locked the door from the stair side.

They that had been following him, ran to the edge of the balcony saying.

"We would have heard him jumping, quickly get him!"

They ran toward the opening of the aqua tanks that led into the aquarium.

"He could only have gone in here. I say, we follow him. You still have your wetsuit on, I have clothing on?"

The guy with the wetsuit did not look impressed and stared down into the waters.

"Is your pistol loaded?"

He nodded and then lowered himself into the clear water, whispering.

"Shoot him and mean to kill him, we've got the Serum formula!"

The man dressed in the wetsuit, while holding his face under the water stared to see what was waiting for him. When he came up for air his accomplice announced.

"You're useless, what are you afraid of?"

"We'll get you Kevin, you cannot stay under, too long!" The guy with the clothes on then exclaimed in pure determination, jumping into the water.

Hardly had they gone to a lower depth, when through the window, Kevin was seen in the laboratory. As it happened, Kevin had been waiting for them to see him and hoped that one of them would be stupid enough to shoot him from the aqua tank. He made for the door but before he could get out, shots started to ring from the inside of the aquarium. Hardly had he locked the sealing doors, using his watch, when he heard the glass windows of the aqua tank shatter.

Almost two floor levels of aquarium emptied, crashing through the glass, while taking the two men as if by some vacuum and spitting their bodies out of the tank, knocking them through the shattered glass into the lab, against the far wall. Kevin knew with the pressure and breaking glass, two men did not stand a chance of survival. Kevin made his way slowly back to the island, although limping to get to the boat.

When Chrystal saw that Kevin was missing, all she could think was, that an undercurrent had swept him, out to sea. A search was called but she could not help crying, saying to David.

"It's not fair, I waited my whole life for him and we've only become engaged!"

David did not know how to comfort her but he knew Kevin would have said to him.

"Be positive, be strong and don't allow your hope to ever die!"

And over and over, he reassured her.

"Be positive, be strong and don't allow your hope to ever die!"

She did say.

"He was a strong swimmer though!"

They stayed on the beach until after dusk. Dark clouds were collecting on the horizon. Chrystal stared out, hoping and praying that Kevin would be all right but she could not stop crying. It was when a light from a motor boat headed straight to the island that she grabbed onto David's arm, without saying a word.

"Ouch, Chrystal!" David cried but understood immediately what she meant and stared silently, out at the nearing light.

Within 15 minutes, the boat was close enough and when away from rocks, sped right up onto the sand.

She was cupping her hands over her mouth, when he looked up and demanded.

"Help me!"

The first that was over the shock of seeing Kevin was David and he ran to the boat, stretched out his arms to his father. Running toward Kevin, Chrystal put out her arms too and so they helped Kevin out of the boat.

"Your foot is badly swollen!" She insisted.

While hugging Kevin, David asked.

"Dad, how the hell did you get where you were?"

By the end of the night, Kevin lay with his foot bandaged and David and Chrystal were laughing, saying.

"How the hang could those guys have tried to shoot through the glass. And thank heaven the fish had fled the action, to lower floors!"

"Well, proudly I must admit that I cannot do too much with my fists but my brain does not stand back for anyone!"

This sent David into a roar of laughter and he patted Kevin on the back saying,

"I'm proud of you, Dad!"

It was in the two days that Kevin spent with his foot lifted, that he pulled the laptop closer. When he had finished his notes much later on, he called Chrystal to lay in his arm and he explained to her.

"We need to get our island seriously going again and I have thought up ways to start up small businesses for the islanders to make a living, thereby being able to stay on the island and enjoy its beauty!"

He went on to say, this part of the island that is so beautiful with the waterfall and streams, we should allow to be natural with hiking trails into the mountains!"

Chrystal soothed.

"Wow that is really something!"

She pointed to something on the other side of the map, just a way from the houses and beach saying.

"Looks like a strip of boxes, what's with the boxes?"

"Every businessman is allowed to have one of these stands. So they can do business and bring in income to keep their families!"

"So what do they do with a stand?"

"I'm going to setup each one with an undercover stall that they themselves could operate. I will also help them with an amount to get started!"

"That is so great. We will be attracting tourists like flies!"

"Yes, thus we have to have a variety of stalls and products!"

She again pointed with her finger to a piece of land, asking.

"And that?"

"Hot houses, we can grow for export different orchids and many other plants!"

"And these little boxes just away from the houses?"

"Offices and small businesses, so we need not get everything from the nearest city!"

"Oops, big box here?"

"Land for the growing of vegetables and fruit!"

"And the box with the stripes right by the side of the land!"

"Factory for laying in and packing etc. of the veggies and fruit!"

"So who makes all the decisions as to what goes where and how it's run?"

"I reckon we should call in all the Islanders and make decisions together and a few persons could be above, these persons!"

Chrystal now turned to him, looked him squarely in the eye and demanded.

"Have you ever told me, I have good taste?"

"In what specifically?"

"Choosing a brilliant man to marry!"

He bounced up from the bed and locked the bedroom door, saying.

"No, but I'm going to show you!"

At that moment his ankle played up and he ended up walking back to the bed with a limp.

"Don't worry, I won't be asking you to walk, anywhere!"

"The bed rest is not working without you, at my side in bed!"

"Take a painkiller!"

"I did, I took three!" He said while seating himself on the bed and rubbing the ankle!"

"Hold it right there!" Chrystal demanded and left for a shower.

When she came out of the shower, she stood in the doorway, while leaning against the wall and asked.

"This sexy enough for you?"

She had on a very see though black negligee. It reached just below her navel. She also wore a very tiny black G-string and a suspender belt that held up dark, sheer stockings. She was proud of the very high stilettos.

"Hey!" She called.

"I'm waiting?"

But alas this time Kevin from the pain medication, was snoring.

Once lying in bed, she sent every selfie to Kevin's mobile. Chrystal felt good.

"Will teach you to take three painkillers, at once!"

She threw her arms around him, snuggling into his closeness and fell asleep, content.

In the morning light, Chrystal rose and slipped into the kitchen she made a great breakfast of bacon and eggs with toast, orange juice and coffee. When the tray was set before Kevin, he woke, breathing hard.

"Flip, what smells so great?"

It was while having his breakfast that he pulled the mobile closer and checked his inbox. Kevin sat suddenly upright, turned his head and stared at her lying at his side, before turning the phone away and flipping through the photos. He demanded.

"Is this you or is someone playing a joke on

me?”

“Oh that!”

She wore a naughty smile, while stating.

“You were sleeping when I came to bed, so I thought of leaving a reminder of what, you had missed last night!”

“Come here!”

“Wait!” She screeched with laughter.

“Let me take the tray away first and use the bathroom!”

“Oh, my soul, here we go again. I hope I’m not asleep by the time you decide to get here!”

Within five minutes, she was standing against the bathroom wall, saying.

“Are you awake this time?”

He rose from the bed saying.

“Do you know that you are the most beautiful woman, I have ever loved?”

She giggled. He started to kiss her, allowing his hands to smooth over the stockings.

As it happened Chrystal had a few consultations and was out, it was a stunning day on the island and when Kevin answered the mobile and his brother James, informed him flatly.

"She's in Venice, Kevin!"

Adding too.

"The divorce will just have to lie a short while longer but I'll finalize as soon as she moves into our territory. At the moment, I'm having her watched so when she arrives, I can do my job!"

"Thanks. Keep me posted on her where about James, my Emma was kidnapped and I'm going to get her back, somehow!"

They spoke on but James too added.

"Do you know where her ladyship is staying? I told you when you wanted to marry her, she only lives in luxury!"

"Where is she staying, James?"

At one of the most luxurious hotels out, The Gondola Palace!"

Should James have put Kevin to this

temptation but Kevin grabbed the opportunity on the spur of the moment, saying to Rick.

"Venice, she's in Venice. Want to come?"

Rick left in a hurry telling.

"I'll see you in a short while!"

Walking to the main bedroom, Kevin pulled a bag from the cupboard, while throwing the necessary clothing into its midst. He waited for Rick to arrive and when Rick introduced the idea of.

"For the sake of costs, I'll pay my way!"

"I'm so angry at Mary for messing up my life, I don't care about costs. I'll stay without food, if I have to!"

"I'll pay the food, Kevin!"

At the airfield, a private plane flew them to Venice and landed on the landing strip of the airport. While looking down to Venice, on landing on airport Marco Polo, Rick amplified.

"Wow. Look at all that emerald water. How the hell will we know where we are, once in a motor boat?"

"Did you know that Venice is sinking five times faster than was thought?" Rick asked.

Kevin laughed, adding.

"Geez. What stunning beauty, I mean the buildings and the arches and peaceful atmosphere. Thanks Rick for spoiling that for me!"

"It's supposed to be the city of romance. Talking of romance did you let your other half know, where you are?"

And Rick went quiet for a while after Kevin had nodded, before he stated.

"Byron would have wanted to take out his canvas and paint, trying to capture this beauty, to keep forever alive!"

Guilt filled Kevin's being and he wondered if his David were to be killed, how he would have felt.

"Does this guilt get any lighter, if I confesses?" He thought to himself.

They left the plane on the landing strip and went straight from there onto a gondola and while on the boat amongst buildings, that filled one with a nostalgia, Rick laughed, saying.

"Shit, look at that, we cannot afford to stay at the Gondola Palace. We'll have to settle for something a little more in our price range!"

"Look that place there, is a little below, what we can afford!"

Kevin added.

"I think we must treat ourselves, just this once and stay at the Gondola Palace. And I'm as hungry as a bear. Let's go straight to the dining room, how's that for style?"

"Well, I'm hungry too but afraid as a chicken to see the menu!" Rick enthused.

It is from The Gondola Palace, that Kevin let Chrystal know where he was.

When Chrystal immediately informed Philip of Kevin's where about, she was totally dismayed, reminding.

"According to you, I am not allowed to tell Kevin about you and me working together and that there are other people involved, so as to keep him thinking that he is, the only one who's saving Emma and this will keep him on track, you say, positive and motivated, but there, he's packed up. Thinks he can do it on his own and I am useless!"

"Steady on now Sis, he never told anyone, he is going. The contact that told him where Mary's, was probably someone, he really trusted. Just threw clothes into a case and off he went to The Gondola Palace, of all places. Probably thought he could only afford to go alone!" And Philip laughed but soothed.

"Stop worrying Chrystal. He is a grown man!"

"What of a back-up Philip. Mary will kill him without hesitation?"

"He's thrown my plans of protecting Emma and her baby slightly haywire. We but we want all Mary's contact's names. This is the main reason we haven't taken Emma yet. This is vital that we know all the contacts. It was with great trust the various countries that have trusted us for delivering to them, all the names. We cannot stop this operation now, it is in the middle of what we have set out to do, in the first place. There was and will be have been numerous opportunities, where we could have taken Emma and disappeared and there will be more. We have an obligation to our friends in the other countries. For, who for them, it is also a matter of importance that this stays under cover, as long as possible. I did not want

Emma to know of anything going on, until the last. Firstly, she is pregnant and must not experience stress and trauma. Secondly if they have to capture her, I mean she'll sing to keep herself and the baby safe!"

Chrystal sounded hysterical now.

"I'm going to join Kevin, right now!"

"Sis, we have enough people that are watching Mary's every move, we don't know who she's going to see next. The contact's names will be delivered to the various agencies, our main job is that Kevin and Rick's mission is to keep Mary moving, worried, so that she can lead us to where her next client is, and in which countries, after all they are all in on the deal. Her deals. I'm sure my men will pick up if Kevin is in danger. These people are in contact with me, all the time!"

She stayed quiet for a long moment and Philip was not sure if she was sulking and he spoke again.

"Crystal, promise me that you will wait for me to give you the go ahead for us to leave and join them, once the plan has come together. That woman is so devious, we cannot for one moment trust her with the unborn child. But we will keep her, Emma as safe as can be. We have a plan of action for when things can go wrong. We have nearly lost them a few times but the backup was always a trusted source!”

“Backup? You mean every country has the backup in place?”

Philip answered.

“Yes Sis, I’ve done my homework this time because it’s family!” He also added.

“Okay!”

“I feel a better!” Chrystal enthused.

“But if you need me, you know where I am!” Chrystal sighed adding.

“Okay!” She started.

“Just let me know what is going on and I’ll let you know what Kevin is up to!”

When going for supper, Rick and Kevin were totally in awe of The Gondola Palace as it rose, like the other stone palaces rose, from the waters, welcoming them from where it overlooked the Grand Channel which seemingly flowed from out of nowhere, but was set within the crisp spring, air in Venice. The Gondola Palace stood nestled, reaching high against and within the space of the buildings floating, from the water. It could well have been added, counting as one of the wonders of the world with its setting arising from along the Grand Canal. Inside it displayed only splendor, with huge guilt edged mirrors, hanging on every wall. The lush of the carpets brought one a feeling of calm and tranquility but its enormity roused your spirit, at every nook and cranny, where valuable artefacts displayed everywhere. The smell of fresh floral bouquets, filled one's being and were seen, as they filled the space and air with their fragrance. Well, that was except for the restaurant area, where in the show fridges, cheeses were on display. It smelled of grilled steaks and cuisine that were at the order of the day.

"Geez, I'm hungry!" Rick amplified again.

"You had better tame that appetite!" Kevin instructed with a smile but disclosed.

"I think we should only eat one in three

meals!”

Rick look disgusted.

“Oh, okay then, let us go in and see what we can afford!”

When Rick was finished eating, he asked in serious tone.

“Do you think we could ask for doggy bags?”

“I don’t know if that would be etiquette but seeing we will only be able to afford every third meal, let us try and feel the waiter about doggy bags?”

Laughing out loud now, Rick amplified so only Kevin could hear.

“I’ll feel him about the matter, you watch his facial reaction and decide if we would feel free to ask?”

When the waiter was standing next to him, Kevin insisted.

“May we have the left-over food, to go please?”

The waiter looked from his menu pad and stared at the food before he looked if there was another waiter around, to order for this task. When they left the restaurant, Rick while wearing a grin, said.

"We're not coming to eat here again. Plenty of other cheaper places with the same food!"

Kevin added.

"Was that not what I said in the first place? The food was amazing and there was enough for two meals, though. So you have your doggy bag and so do I. I'm stuffed for the moment!"

"Did you see his face when we asked for doggy bags?"

"I know!"

He laughed. By late afternoon they were back in the suite and there was a knock on the door. The door handle turned and a woman walked in, saying.

"Hi. Philip sent me. I'm here to do your make up!"

"What do you mean?"

The phone rang and Kevin answered.

"I've sent one of my people to disguise you, seeing that you went ahead of us and are actually in grave danger of being killed!"

"Umm. Rick is with me, trying to save costs, sharing!"

"I know that, Chrystal did not!"

Only when she started to do their disguises, Kevin realized of the actual danger he was in, as no one beside Chrystal, knew of this expedition of his, to find Mary and Emma, here in Venice.

"I did not realize Philip's men were so onto Mary!" Kevin acknowledged to Rick.

Staying at The Gondola Palace was to some degree an experience that Emma did not want to exchange but in her heart, she wanted to be with Anton. She wanted to feel his arms around her more than anything. Shopping with Mary became a situation in which Mary was moody because of the business that she was doing and was not closing off deals, as fast as she should have, after her disappearance from the island. Now here at the Gondola Palace, she had promised Emma that they would concentrate on shopping, for baby things and Emma, though looking excited when seeing the pretty things, was homesick and only wanted to laze around the suite, hoping for the time to pass, so she could be with Anton. Emma lately, thought often of her father and Eddy and she still got the glass horse with her. She wanted to share the two people she loved the most in the world, with each other. When she asked Mary.

"When will we see Dad, again?"

Mary pretended to be busy most of the time and thus Emma's question went unanswered, more often than not.

She spoke to Mary although knowing that her mother's thoughts were elsewhere.

"Do you think Dad is going to like Anton, Mom?"

"Mmm!" Mary would reply, while not looking up from what she was doing.

Sometimes Mary would shout at her for asking and Emma really had to fight the dislike, she sometimes inside of her, felt, for her mother. When they started their second days stay, here at The Gondola Palace, Mary in delighted tone, informed.

"Now Emma, this is Lida and she will be your body guard!"

Blushing slightly, Emma smiled at her but

immediately turned to her mother and asked.

"Why do I need a body guard, I just don't understand it!"

"Emma accept it and treat Lida with respect, like one would treat a body guard. She is not your friend to talk our business to, she has a job to do and gets paid to do it well!"

Needless to say Lida and Emma spent much time together and became very good friends. When Emma asked.

"Can we go shopping?" Lida was the one that knew, where all the hotel stores on the bottom landing were.

"Actually Lida, I enjoyed the afternoon shopping with you. You have made a difference to my stay here!"

It was close to The Basilica of Saint Mark, that Lida insisted.

"Only one more store to browse down the road and then I'm going to get you home for a snack and rest!"

"Well, I am tired but I'm having such fun with you!"

In his disguise Kevin walked close behind his daughter. His heart ached to hold her in his arms and take her back with him. He was disappointed when the sound like that of a fire cracker came because it sounded like a gunshot and Lida grabbed Emma by the hand and ran for the hotel lift. When safely in the lift, while the doors were still ajar, a women made her way in too exclaiming.

"Some fool let off an air gun, while he was about to pay for it!"

"What was that running all about?" Emma asked, while her heart was still beating wildly.

"While you are lying down comfortably, I'm going to sit right there by your side and talk to you!"

"Oh, great I'm going to love that and the baby can have his nap inside of me, at the same time!"

Later after lunch and while Emma was having a lie down on the double poster bed, Lida started talking to her.

"Emma, you know you are here on business with your mother. Do you know what business?"

"No idea, my mother is always busy with something!"

"Emma it is better that you don't know!"

Lida thought about how to tell Emma about her mother, but stood up and left the room. She went to her own room and lay down on the bed, while allowing her thoughts to wander off, thinking.

"How could I tell Emma?"

Sleep tugged at her being and Lida started to speak.

"Emma, can I tell you a very big secret, do you promise never to tell or talk to anyone besides me, about it?"

Emma half rose, her eyes were wide, she nodded.

"Emma, your mother is trying to sell you and your baby!"

"Why, why would she do that. It's her grandchild and what about Eddy?"

"We don't know why, actually we do. I'm going to explain to you now. You see your dad on request of your mother, developed a Serum to help people and children, babies that have some brain damage, to be able to use more of their brain, so they can stand up to survival in life!"

Emma nodded saying.

"Yes I know about that. My dad is actually a genius for having developed the serum!"

"The serum fell into the wrong hands. Also your Dad had not finished testing the serum for safety on human use, yet. People, children were being injected with it. The person, the wrong hands it fell into, for the sake of making it work for a lifetime, had added mercury to it. Mercury is deadly if the person was not given anti-serum injections!"

She stopped talking and stayed quiet, giving Emma time to digest the information before she carried on.

"Emma, your baby's father, Eddy, was given the injection containing mercury but your own father saved his life, by giving him the anti-serum, secretly!"

"Eddy, Eddy…"

Emma sat up right now. She swung her legs from the bed and asked.

"Why did no one tell me?" She asked.

"Emma you are going to have to be strong

now. Do you understand that Anton loves you with all his heart?"

"Off course I know that. I love Eddy."

"You must know first of all. Anton and I are undercover agents, looking out and protecting you and your unborn child!"

The room was silent and when Lida spoke again, she confessed.

"I'm Dina from the cabin!"

Emma put her hands to her mouth and took in every part of Dina, looking to recognize her, before exclaiming.

"I see it is you, Geez, you look amazing, even disguised!"

Lida laughed.

"Thanks, but there's more!"

The door opened and Anton came into the room.

He took a few steps and reached his arms around Emma, saying.

"For the sake of the child and for the sake of your love, for the sake of you and Eddy, you have to be strong now, Emma!"

Silence reigned before Emma asked, softly.

"Why, what is going on, I don't understand

what is happening?"

Anton held her tighter, looked deeply into her eyes and said.

"Your mother is trying to sell you and the unborn child for 10 Million dollars. An informant has reported it and we are tracking her every move, to protect you and the child!"

"Is that why she is forcing me to go everywhere with her?"

Anton and Dina nodded.

"That's really not a nice thing to do!" And she started to cry.

Anton reminded.

"You promised me that you are going to be strong for the sake of the baby and you and Eddy!"

She fought back the tears.

"What's going to happen now?"

Anton held her gaze with his, while asking.

"There are a few of us, very trained people that are protecting you. You know I love you too and more than life itself. Can you trust me when I say I'm looking out for you, so is Dina and quite a few others, too. No harm is coming to you. Please, your mother must not know anything. She must not know that we are tracking her or you. She must not know that we have spoken to you!"

Emma nodded and breathed.

"So you don't stay home and wait for me?"

"No, I am everywhere you are!"

He kissed her. Emma wore a new radiance but Anton started to say.

"Your mother injected you with an amnesia injection when she kidnapped you from the island?"

She put her hands to her face and started to cry.

Anton kissed her saying.

"Don't worry about that now. We will sort things out with Eddy!"

Emma put in now.

"I love him so much Anton, I cannot imagine what you are telling me!"

"There is something else and I will let Dina tell you but now I have to disappear. Just remember I am with you and our baby, all over!" He kissed her and left.

Waiting first for Anton to shut the door, Dina made sure that there was no one listening to the conversation, before she started.

"Emma your father has been searching for you and is right here!"

"Wow! that is great news. Daddy. I want him to meet Anton!"

"Now you remember that your mom is not to know about anyone of us protecting you!"

Emma nodded. She was lying with her feet up, relaxing on the bed.

Opening her eyes slightly, Dina tried to wake by dozed off again. Dina was sitting in the comfy chair by her side, when Emma while gathering her thick strawberry colored hair and tying it back roughly, half rose and looked Dina in the eyes and said.

"I'm bored and homesick and I want to be with Eddy!"

In her heart Dina knew that Emma was being serious but gave a small laugh, hoping that the girl would not insist on such request.

"Oh, come on, Dina?" She begged.

"Oh my word, Emma, do you know what this could mean to the whole keeping you and baby safe, project?"

"I don't care, I just know I cannot take another moment of this nonsense from my Mom and the longing, I feel something for Anton!"

She then stared at Dina.

"Oh Darn it, Emma. When you look at me with those puppy dog eyes, I cannot say no!"

Emma sat upright on the bed, her face was radiant and she demanded.

"A CIA plan, please!"

"Geez, now we must think well because you are endangering many people's lives, if this goes wrong!"

"It won't go wrong, I promise, I just want to be with Anton for two hours!"

"Oh my gosh, I could get fired for this and probably Anton too!"

And Dina pulled the cell phone from a hidden pocket below her breast bone on the baggy dress, she wore. She did not greet but whispered into the phone.

"Emma wants to be with you for an hour or so, talks of just wanting you to hold her!"

He did not sound as if he argued once. Dina answered with.

"I told her we could all be fired and, and. Okay at the Gondola entrance to Waters Edge Boulevard!" She repeated.

She gave Emma a look and hid the phone away in her bodice, saying.

"Get ready were going to a movie, you and I!"

Disappointment showed on her face when Emma stared at her without saying anything.

"Don't ask questions, just look sexy!"

Reading now between the lines, Emma giggled and stuck out her baby bump so she looked very pregnant, requesting.

"Sexy enough!"

"Beautiful, counts a hundred times more than sexy Emma, get going!"

When Dina said this there came a knock on the door and Mary entered. Emma's face dropped, she knew Mary was fetching her to show off to some rich client. She was expecting her mother to demand that she go with to wherever she was off to.

"How are you girls?" Mary spoke as if in a hurry, not waiting for them to answer, but adding.

"I'm going to meet with a client, who is having another client sit in for the meeting tonight, I might not be early, so don't wait up!"

In her mind, Emma gave silent thanks.

"Oh, thank you, thank you, for getting Mom out of my hair for tonight!"

Showering quickly and getting herself ready, Emma stated.

"I'm ready!"

But Dina presented her with a brown hooded cape. Emma stared at it, asking.

"You told me to look sexy!"

"Put it on, I'm in trouble if you get seen anywhere!"

They arrived at the Gondola canal that Dina pointed to a waiting Gondola. Anton appeared from over the bridge in the dark. He assisted her into the gondola, safely. He then gave Dina a wink and bid her.

"Enjoy the show!"

In the boat Emma felt safe, she was with the man she loved with her being. The air smelled fresh as the river had currently come down and brought new waters and lapping against the gondola where in the moonlight,

Anton kissed her. The Gondola left for wherever, they did not care and while in his arms, she forgot about everything separating their souls from joining in a flight, toward their destiny. After two hours, Anton gave a small laugh while standing up to help Emma onto the walkway.

"Oops, Dina is already waiting!"

And the evening ended as they went apart. When Emma turned back to give him a longing glance, Dina breathed.

"I hope that time together will last you for a long while!" She giggled and then hooked her arm into Emma's, saying.

"Let's get you home, you have not rested, today!"

Nothing mattered to Emma, she was elated.

Dina was still dreaming even slumbering when she abruptly awoke to the sound of footsteps in her room.

It was Mary who lately was in a bad mood and shortly following her was Emma. Mary stated.

"They're taking advantage of my situation!"

Feeling uncomfortable with Mary in her bedroom, Dina turned inviting.

"Let's sit in the lounge and I'll pour us each a glass of freshly squeezed juice!"

"What do you mean, Mom?" Emma insisted while following the group to the lounge.

Before Mary could answer, Emma turned to Dina and jokingly put in.

"It's like raising Arizona, keeping my mom satisfied with life!"

And then while holding her hand on her hip stared at Mary for a moment, waiting for an answer but within moments went on to say.

"You are just always in a bad mood lately, Mom. I'm too afraid to talk to you!"

"Oh, I'm leaving for my suite, let's have the juice there. In any case you won't understand Emma, don't you worry about my things!"

It was once the last glass was empty that Dina showed with her eyes, for her and Emma to leave to their suite. When having said goodnight to Mary, Emma and Dina left.

In Emma's bedroom, she demanded.

"Dina, did you do this?"

"What?" She asked, while staring at the

necklace, lying on Emma's pillow.

"What?" She repeated.

"This heart with a diamond on a gold chain!"

Emma didn't recognized the pendant her father had given her on her sixteenth birthday. But she placed it around her neck.

Once settled in bed, with curtains opened, she needed the light of the moon to keep reminding her of Anton's touch on her lips. Emma had planned to slumber at a place where she was allowed to be in Anton's arms. But now, sleep eluded her and Emma lay awake for a long time. She thought of the pendant that she was still wearing. Knowing that she knows the pendant but it was a strange feeling to see it lying on the pillow. She thought of Kevin and smiled, remembering back to as a child sitting on his lap, chatting about things she did. She knew Kevin would enjoy Venice and she imagined herself with Kevin, walking to the various curio shops, looking at the lace, the colors and blown glass even the various art of Venice, made here in this city and being one of the best tourist's attractions in the world. She pictured herself in a gown of pearls and diamonds awaiting for the love of her life, Anton. She dreamed of a gondola moving on the water as romantic music from around, played. Light opera sounded and instrumental notes filled a candle lit room, where she, safe in the arms of Anton, held a bouquet of flowers. Anton kissed her where she lay against his shoulder and she slipped away and found herself at the waterfall, in awe drinking in a feeling of warmth spiraling with love to fill her very being. Emma closed her eyes and Kevin's image came up in her mind. She smiled with the thought of sitting on his lap and talking to him about everyday things. She knew that Kevin would've enjoyed Venice and she imagined herself and Kevin, walking to the various curio shops in the ground floor of nearly each building and looking at the lace, glass and various art of Venice that made this city one of the best tourist's attractions in the world. She imagined herself in a stunning gown of pearls and diamonds awaiting her Eddy. She dosed off and dreamed of the romantic scenes where she and Eddy were in a gondola, slowly moving on the water, as romantic music filled the air from above. She closed her eyes to the light opera and calming instrumental music in a candle lit room. She was safe in Anton's arms now.   Anton passed the bouquet of flowers to her as he kissed her on the pier, where on the gondola, she slumbered against his shoulder and fell asleep in the arms of the love of her life. The waterfall appeared and a feeling of warm love filled her very being.

In her bedroom, Mary lay alone in the big double bed but sleep too eluded her. She went over her catch phrase, over and over.

"You will possess the first brilliant, the world has ever seen. I also present you with the formula for incubating more brilliants, for the future!"

While in bed, Mary sounded adamant when she demanded of herself.

"What the hell am I doing wrong? Why am I given such low offers, I mean 10 Million Dollars is nothing, compared to their riches!"

Another sleepless night followed, she while she went over the offer she was making the client now, for introducing her to another client. A percentage would then be given to the one introducing her to the next client, if the deal be closed.

It was again the following evening when Mary came home late saying.

"I have not closed the deal, we'll be staying another day or two!"

"Oh Mom, I want to go back home, I'm longing for Eddy, to be with him but fine, I still have not bought a few things for the baby, which I will do now!"

"I'm going to bed, see you in the morning Emma!" Mary disclosed and left for her suite.

It was late night, Emma heard the fidgeting at the front door of the suite but ignored it, as being her imagination, playing up.

And then while shouting at Dina, amplified.

"Someone tried to break in and Lida, I hold you responsible that you did not hear it, you are here to protect us, or at least help protect us?"

"Lida was with me, Mom. We were awake?"

"Well, pack up then, we're leaving for home and Lida, this cheque is for you, for your services. Thank you, you're fired!"

She swing on her heel to Emma informing.

"My next client appointment leaves us with time to go back to the Swiss Alps!"

The suite was unlocked and deserted. Disappointed, he left back to his room, not thinking that the security would have recognized him in the disguise, but he had hardly turned to leave and four men appeared from behind him. Kevin ran, hoping to make it to the suit. Rick was following him closely but when the four men that chased them, overtook Rick throwing him to the ground and chased after Kevin. Two of the men forced him to the basement and then started, beating him up and kicking him. He, Kevin tried to stand up, just to be his ribs cracked when he was kicked in the ribs again. There was a sound of footsteps coming from the stairs which sent the two men to hide behind the door. It gave Kevin time and he took the opportunity to rise to his feet and he sped out of the room into the passage way. The two men tried to keep a low profile and stay from sight but gave chase. Kevin used every spurt of energy and he ran for the buildings foyer and into the walkway. Glancing back over his shoulder he found that the two men were still tagging him. He turned right into the following walkway but on immediately taking another left turn Kevin's foot slipped on the wet cement and he fell hard against the pavement landing and almost hitting his head on the wall of a small curio shop.   He regained his balance immediately, while people were stopping to stare but now the two men had reached him and without warning Kevin was pulled by his shirt front and hit full in the face. This sent him tilting neck back to fall over backwards. He lay dead still. Meanwhile the other was coming towards Kevin with unusual speed and Kevin reached out his fist and hit him full in the jaw. Stunned too for the moment at the blow he gave, Kevin shook at his painful fist before he made a fast getaway to the bridge.

Hardly had he become aware of the peace within the place when the assailant following him pulled a pistol from his pocket and pointed it at Kevin. To Kevin it felt as though he was staring death in the face as the assailant was so close that all Kevin could do was lift his hands in submission. The assailant did not quite have that in mind and hit Kevin to fall onto the hard stone of the bridge. At that very moment the assailant kicked him hard in the ribs. It was when Kevin rolled away and stood up fast his gaze met that of the assailant and while holding onto the painful place he had just been kicked, Kevin threw himself forward while pushing the man against the stone wall of the bridge. He was pointing the pistol with a silencer on into Kevin's face. Kevin cried.

"Wait, wait, and wait!" To Kevin it felt as if the end has come. He could feel the blood pumping into his head and closed his eyes, waiting. It was when he heard the shot and he did not feel anything that Kevin slowly opened his eyes. He looked down to his chest, expecting to see blood. He stood astounded to look into the wide open eyes of the man holding the pistol, as he fell backwards and into the river. Allowing his gaze to drink in any movement around him, Kevin breathed.

"Not a soul, how the hell did that happen?"

He turned to see the man floating face down in the water. Kevin turned and started walking back to the hotel but collapsed as he walked into their suite. Kevin felt safer but not at peace because he wanted his daughter safe and with him. No matter what. Probably tonight was no matter what.

When Kevin awoke it was in much pain, in a hospital bed. He asked for Chrystal to be contacted and after the nursing staff had explained to her in what condition, Kevin found himself. He spoke to Chrystal in pleading tone.

"I love you my Chrystal!"

He knew she was angry for him packing up and leaving without her, but now he knew she did have reason.

She finished speaking to Kevin and immediately phoned Philip. She spoke sternly.

"If it were not for some kindly soul who shot the two assailants, Kevin might not have made it. He is to stay in hospital for a few days. Reason one, as one of his ribs punctured his lung and I want to leave immediately to be at his side!"

"Kevin must head back home as soon as he can and take some time off and get well. My agent has let me know, Emma and Mary are on their way for rest in Switzerland. Do not allow Kevin to know this fact, as he will then interfere, where I have a head office and the best men around the clock are working on the case. We have to give Mary rope, so we can track the clients she is now, dealing with. But under no circumstances until she is trapped, allow him to go to Switzerland, Sis, he will be messing up a perfect operating plan that is in place, to get Mary and every corrupt person around and off course, saving more children from getting hurt!"

"Okay, I'm leaving to him immediately and we'll be home as soonest!" She breathed.

When Chrystal arrived at the hospital, she

found Kevin still looking pale.

Kevin told her about the two men chasing him and how the one was shot by an unknown assailant. Chrystal was perturbed, she was thankful for her fiancé's miraculous escape and planned on discussing the whole episode with Philip.

In hospital, Kevin reached for his phone, wincing some but while staring at him, Chrystal passed it to him. It was Philip and they spoke. Chrystal heard Kevin explain about the man being shot on the bridge and found out that it was one of Philip's men and much later when Kevin placed down the phone, he informed Rick.

"Were going home for a short while, one, so I can re cooperate and two, Philip wants to be sure of where Mary is!"

Knowing she hated lies, especially lying to her husband to be but as people's lives were at stake, she dared not tell Kevin that Mary and Emma were in Switzerland. The solution, Chrystal found it easier than lying, was to just say nothing at all.

"Since his youngest days, he has been

impulsive where it comes to things that lay close to his heart and Emma, closer than close!"

She thought about the matter and decided.

"In any case, Kevin needs to rest and heal. There are those of Philip working full time on the case, it'll be okay to wait for her next move!"

She also remembered that.

"At least she is not seeing clients in Switzerland, so Emma for the moment is safe!"

Chrystal debated this all to herself, while the cake mixer was whizzing, at high speed.

"Chocolate cake for the arrival of the man in my life, is my way of saying, I love you and I'm so glad you're home!"

"I am going to ice this onto the chocolate cake!"

With music blaring and the smell of cake baking in the oven, Chrystal took out the icing set from the cupboard.

"Cute!" She exclaimed taking the shape from the box.

"Going to write the words in icing on the

cake with this pencil like thing of the icing set!"

It was exactly a half hour later, when she moaned.

"Frick it, could they not have made the thing, automatic? The blue icing sugar is all over, my hand is slipping on the icing machine, actually no, it is in excruciating cramp and I've shot blobs of blue icing against the walls!"

Chrystal did persevere though and ending up with the message, Welcome home though the "Welcome" fell off the cake as she only managed to get on to the top of the cake, "Welco" and eventually took a knife and smeared it, taking the words away, but she tried again. By the time she placed the cake into the holder, she said.

"Frikkit not playing housewife to that extent again. Will buy a cake next time!"

On arriving back on the island, from hospital in France, Rick dropped Kevin at his home. Kevin immediately demanded a slice of chocolate cake, before supper, in the kitchen that smelled of it. On Chrystal presenting a large slice, he smiled, saying.

"Ah, my favorite, chocolate cake with white and blue marbling effect, like she wrote something on the cake and wiped it in. Just what the doctor ordered!" He studied her for a moment, before he added.

"My Chrystal. Never wanted to be a housewife, just a career woman and now she's writing book pages of messages, on the chocolate cake!"

Determined not to tell him about her failed effort at writing on the cake, she let him be.

Kevin took a big bite and on closing his eyes, soothed.

"Mmmm! Best cake made with love, that I have ever tasted!"

She threw her arms around him and said.

"That's all that matters!"

He added though.

"Well, I just read it as the blue and white marbling went down!"

She laughed now, asking.

"What did it say, tell me what I wrote?"

He showed to his mouth and pretended, it to being full and through its fullness, said.

"Can't!" And he pointed to the slice of cake.

When he had finished eating, he placed down the plate. She had been waiting for him to finish and demanded.

"Tell me what I wrote?"

He laughed aloud and pulled her into his arms saying.

"Dear Kevin, I love you very much and I'm so glad you're home and have wondered if you forgot, that in our student days, I wanted a locket with a heart on and inside, I wanted to put a photo of you and me!"

Kevin then reached into his pocket and pulled the small long box out, saying.

"Off course, I remember my darling and I give it to you now, with all my love!"

Her face lit up when she opened the box and when seeing the fine gold locket, that lay sparkling inside, she amplified.

"Kevin I am speechless!" She went on, though.

"I don't know what to say, oh heck, what have I done so right, to deserve you!"

Was it guilt but she also explained.

"I tried my hand at icing, saying, welcome home, I love you and this is my way of saying it!"

He laughed aloud and enthused.

"Message experienced and I know you love me. I can't boil an egg but I can remember!" And he pointed to the locket, saying.

"Open it!"

She did open it and without saying a word, stared hard at the inside. There within the safety of the front and back joined hearts was a photo of them, Chrystal and Kevin in each other's arms, back in their student days.

"Oh gosh, it is so amazing, I don't know what to say but thank you!"

She leaned in and started to kiss him.

She ordered.

"While you shower, I'll put my locket away and get you a nice cup of tea!"

He spoke.

"And a piece of your marble cake!"

"I'm going to get you for saying that!"

"Please don't, I'm not ready to be mauled!"

As Chrystal turned and made for the kitchen, he spoke.

"Don't forget my marble cake?"

She stopped dead, turned and rushed after him and when he fell onto the bed, Chrystal unloosed his shirt buttons, one for one. Then she said.

"Now Kevin, you know that you are already in pain, but seeing you were challenging me to do this, I am forced to put you on your place!"

They were both laughing aloud now, she went on to say.

"Notice that I am sitting on your hip bones, so as not to cause extra pain!"

He replied through laughter.

"Yes!"

"Well do you notice that when my lips meet yours like that!"

And she started to kiss him gently.

"That there is no pain!"

He now was over the laughing stage, in his mind things had gotten serious but she carried on.

"So if I had to remove your clothing gently, I would do it like that and was that painful, now?"

She waited for him to answer. Kevin laughed again but shook his head.

"But if I, from my side, found it in my heart, to do this to help you, like this, would it be all right?"

She started kissing him, asking.

"Mm, what do you say?"

"Oh Shit, just cut the crap and do it!" Kevin pleaded.

"Oh and now, how's the pain when you command me?"

She started laughing now, loving him like he had never been loved before and when he asked her to stop for a moment, she took the opportunity, to give him all of her.

Afterwards when they lay quietly, she breathed.

"That was saying thanks for the locket!"

"Oh. Okay. Does it count if I did not hear it, could you say it again?"

"Geez. Just give me two hours to recuperate, please?"

Being back on the island with Chrystal, was a relief for Kevin and it was later the same evening, when he suggested.

"Feel like a shower?"

"How can you ask?"

In the shower when Kevin pulled her close and the soapy warmth of their bodies touched, he could not help but go above the pain, putting both arms around her and while cupping her with his hands, he lifted her to him and when the water was already cooling, they spoke for the first time. Kevin was getting out from the shower.

"Shall we sit in the gazebo for a while and just listen to the crickets and insects, making music?"

"Sounds great. I'll make a plate of cheese snacks, if you pour two whiskeys!" She sounded.

The night was lit up by a waxen moon and

Kevin in the gazebo, pulled her into his arms, although cringing slightly until she was comfortable, against him. While sitting quietly, an owl hopped into their view. Chrystal gave a slight start, saying.

"He is so big, I thought he looked like a very large cat!"

Giving a small laugh, Kevin did not say anything but watched the owl and the owl watched them, even rotating it's head all the way around. When he flew off, Chrystal breathed.

"Is life not simply amazing, here on the island?"

But Kevin placed down the empty glass and invited her.

"The whiskey and lemonade have anesthetized me. Let's go to bed?"

She laughed, gathered the tray and walked ahead of him into the house.

It was days after Kevin had arrived back on the island and the motor boat, he had ordered was still waiting for their attention, since delivery when he asked.

"What say you, we take the boat out?"

"Yay Kevin, I'd love it!" She replied and Chrystal in delight threw down everything she was doing.

"Well, let's get to the harbor and pull her out, then!"

"David seeing you are going to friends later on, well see you when you get back!"

They walked to the small harbor, carrying the basket of food between them.

"What a really stunning day. It all seems too good to be true when one sees the beauty of the gardens and plants around us. It is just rather quiet, I'm missing the chirping of birds. Look around us, I don't see birds!" Chrystal spoke.

Deep in thought, Kevin carried on toying with his thoughts.

He did speak eventually saying.

"We can just quietly drift along the coastline, not far off from the shore!"

She loved the warmth of the sun on her body and Chrystal had only sat down in the boat, after saturating herself with oil and protection cream. They returned home and find Philip in the lounge. His face was serious and he started talking.

"We have to let Eddy and Emma talk. It's vital now that she has support and that she knows it."

"How?" Kevin enquired.

The "bodyguards left something for Emma under the glass horse. We will get a message to her to use it to make contact. We unfortunately cannot be on the island when we do this. We must be much closer. We found the cabin in Switzerland and we have to get close enough for the signal to work. We have to take Eddy with this time and I'm sure he is packed and ready, because I left him a message of our plan."

"Brilliant, and well thought out." Chrystal confirmed.

Philip continued.

"We will be leaving in two days. A helicopter will take us to the airport where we will board a private plane and then we're off to Switzerland."

Kevin said.

"For Emma…"

Chrystal confirmed.

"For Emma…and the baby…always."

Two days later the plane was ready and they were flying to Switzerland. It was mid-summer in Switzerland and the flight was beautiful to see nature in its full capacity and beauty.

Eddy was sitting at the window and asked where they were and if they're close.

"We're nearly there," the pilot announced.

Eddy's eyes lit up and Kevin and Chrystal could see the love in his eyes for Emma. Kevin knew that Emma and Eddy will be together one day. Shortly.

At the airport they were met by Philip and a lady. She explained that they went to the cabin when no one was there and that they had made adjustments to the glass horse so that Eddy and Emma could talk for the first time in months.

Not far from the cabin, another cabin was rented to make the contact possible. It was now just to find the right time and place to do this. Not far from the cabin was a waterfall and they've asked Emma to be there if she could. All she had to do is to press a small button at the side of the horse and the signal will be sent to the cabin. When exactly no one knew because Mary was nearly every minute at her side. She must make a time and she will determine the exact date and time when they would be able to talk. It wasn't going to establish contact and everyone hoped for the best.

Kevin, Chrystal, Philip and Eddy would make turns every day to see if the signal came through. They did not know when so they were on duty 24 hours. This will be divided by four and each one of them will get a certain time to be on duty. Philip said it would be better if they do it in 12 hour shifts so that at least they will get enough time to rest. They will be in the cabin the whole time until the contact was established and Emma was okay for them to leave. They knew that this could take a couple of months and they knew it could take a couple of days. Now that Emma knew that Mary was up to other sinister plans will make her anxious and Eddy was there to support and the others too, but Eddy was the priority.

Arriving at the cabin they were deep up in the mountains. Philip explained.

"One room is smaller than the other and is equipped with the best electronic devices we could find. We even had to invent a way for the horse to transmit, so we replaced it with invisible (it looks like glass) cables and devices that can transmit to out room. It was definitely one of the most intricate operations we've ever done like this. We had to find a lot of things and turn them "into glass" and to make them untraceable because Mary also has her way of sweeping the cabin once a week. This could be a good time for Emma to try and make contact, all depends on where Mary is at that moment because she rarely gives Emma time on her own. She cannot go out by night because the cameras will see her go out. Her security is now very tight and the only thing we can do is to trust Emma with the timing of this. I cannot guarantee that she's going to make contact, but I know that she desperately want to.

Anton is there for her protection and he knows about this. They could probably make a plan together and sneak away for an hour or so. Any questions?"

Eddie asked. "Can I see the waterfall?"

"I'll take you there." Philip answered.

"How close are we?" It was Eddy again.

"Close enough for contact." Phillip replied.

"We cannot compromise the agents in the house and most of all, Emma's safety at this stage. This is a shot in the dark…we don't know the outcome yet. Don't go to the waterfall ever again after I've showed you where it is. That will blow the whistle for Mary."

"I promise I won't put everything in jeopardy." Eddy promised.

"Now, Eddy I have to blindfold you to take you to the waterfall. Let's go." Philip demanded.

"Hundred percent." Eddy complied.

As they drove Eddy lay down on the backseat and it was about a half an hour later that they stopped. They walked for about

twenty minutes and Phillip said that he could take off the blindfold. Eddy looked at the waterfall in awe. He was struck with the beauty and the similarity of the water fall in 29. He walked around and swam in the pool. The water was as cold as ice but he was content and at peace. They returned to the cabin and Kevin and Chrystal already unpacked and they were busy with dinner.
Day by day they sat at the receiver but it never gave the green light. It's been a week and there was no contact yet.

In Mary's cabin it was also peaceful and she was phoning her contacts to make appointments for her and Emma. Emma was never out of her sight and she made sure that she kept her close by.
One day when the cabin was to be swept, Emma asked Mary if she and Anton could take a walk but Mary refused. Emma took Anton's hand in hers and she asked again. Mary stared at them and Anton made a

gesture that it will be okay. Mary said that they could only go as far as the pond, not far from the cabin. She was looking at them the whole time and saw that Anton and Emma was kissing each other. She felt more at ease knowing that Anton was there to protect Emma. Every night Emma kissed the horse and she made sure that she knew where to press if she wanted to make contact. She desperately needed to hear Eddy's voice. One day Mary said that she was going to town to talk to someone and she needed Emma to stay. Emma asked.

"Mom…"

Mary looked at Emma.

"Yes my dearest Emma."

Emma continued.

"Can Anton and I go to the waterfall close by?"

Anton was standing right next to her and Mary's eyes softened. Suddenly Emma saw her real Mom again. Emma shouted…

"Thank you Mom, thank you…"

Mary couldn't refuse and she got into her car and drove off.

Immediately Emma went to her room and put the horse under her jacket and went out. Anton was still waiting. They reached for each other's hands and started walking to the waterfall.

Mary was calm as soon as she saw they took hands and she was confident to leave them for the next two hours.

It was quite a walk to the waterfall and an hour later they've reached the waterfall.

Emma asked.

"I need time alone and went and sit at the edge of the water. Pressed the button and within seconds Eddy answered.

"Emma I love you."

"I love you too…you're going to be a daddy." Emma replied.

"Are you okay and how is she treating you?" Eddy wanted to know.

"She is treating me fine and I think we only have a few minutes left. It took us more than an hour to get here. But I'm going to leave the horse here for you. It gave me hope and it's going to give you hope too." Emma concluded.

"Thank you and your Dad and Chrystal is sending their love and remember I love you always. Take care. See you soon." Eddy's voice broke.

"Love you too…" Emma put the horse into the water where she sat and she had now a lot more confidence and peace in her heart. She walked back to Anton and took his hand and as they returned Mary was driving towards the cabin and saw them walk hand in hand. She smiled and as she got out of the car she told them to prepare for a trip to Casa Blanca the next day. She went into the house and they didn't see her for the rest of the day. She stayed in her room, talking on her phone.

Eddy ran to Philip and told him they must go to the waterfall. This time he wasn't blindfolded and he ran to the water's edge and started looking for the horse. After about 15 minutes of looking he saw the horse laying in the shallow end of the pool. He picked it up and held it against his chest. He started to cry out loud and Philip came and put his arm around his shoulders and comforted him. He was crying the whole time until they reached the cabin. He went to the stream and washed his face. He was eternally grateful for being able to talk to her and he knew he gave her strength and peace as well.

The contact was made and Philip said that they had to leave immediately. As they drove off, Eddy looked back and saw a crew starting to demolish the cabin and he knew that this was only a temporary cabin, just for him and Emma.

He said.
"Philip, I want to thank you for this opportunity. Please tell everyone involved that they've changed our lives forever today. This day we will remember forever.
Philip nodded and said.
"I will."
Eddy looked at Philip's eyes in the mirror and saw him wipe a tear off his cheek.

Within a few hours they were back on the plane and heading for the island.

4 CASABLANCA

The private plane belonging to a client of Mary was already gearing for a descent, while circling the airport. Sitting at Mary's side, Emma enthused.

"How long are we going to stay here?"

"I hate that question Emma and I know you're asking as you want to go back to the cabin. We are staying for a week, so accept it and do shopping!"

Neither the neatness of Casablanca nor the architecture could hold Emma spellbound at this moment. For Emma being in love was taxing on the human mind. Mary had spoken and Emma knew Mary will go out of her way to keep her word, as she always reminds.

"To teach you to appreciate what I do for you!" The pilot was telling them of Casablanca while he made his way to a safe landing.

"This city created in Moorish style one could not believe, was totally destroyed by an earth quake in 1755. Casablanca means, white house in Spanish!"

The intercom sounded on, while Mary stretched

over past Emma to see the city through the window. The pilot spoke.

"The most famous landmark of Morocco and Casablanca is the Mosque Hassan II, if you look below you will immediately recognize it with the description, I give you.

It was built from donations in 1986-1989 by the ruler King Hassan and it cost 800 Billion Dollars to build. 25 hundred construction workers and 10 000 artists, among other participated in the building, décor and the design of the Hassan II. Adorning the inside, 50 tons of glass chandeliers have been used. It was built from White granite and inside there are 78 columns of pink granite in the hall of prayer. Off course only the best flooring can for such dynamic building, be in order and gold marble and green onyx, were used for this purpose. The roof as you can see is covered with bright emerald shingles. And note well please, it has a retractable roof and heated floors. This building is also earthquake proof. Take note that the Minarette that is pointing at us above the Mosque, has a 30 metre lazer beam and the light of it, is directed at The Sacred Mosque in Mecca which is the largest. All Mosques have, distinctive minarettes.

The Hassan 2 Mosque dominates Casablanca!"
Mary spoke now saying.

"Emma the Mosque, the Hassan II is almost on the beach, so close to nature and away from the bustle, it overlooks the sea. Do you know when designing it, a verse in the Koran was taken in mind. The verse being:

"Allah's home is on the water!"

So the Hassan II Mosques is built above the water level, of the Atlantic Ocean. Now at high tide, when praying in the mosque, one has a feeling of floating above the water!"

Adding though, Mary stated.

"Can probably be seen from afar!"

"Okay!" Emma sounded flatly.

The Captain again spoke.

"The Hassan II Mosque stands on 9 Hectare of ground, full and as I said, is the second largest mosque in the world. Do you see the Minaret as it reaches 210 meters to the heavens? It is the tallest religious structure in the world!"

He stopped talking for a moment, checked the gauges and spoke again into the intercom.

"And with that I bid you a safe stay in Casablanca, Miss Mary and Miss Emma!"

The hotel courtesy car was waiting to fetch them

and Mary and Emma were guided like VIP's, safely into the hotel.

When reaching their suite at the hotel, Mary felt guilty for being so hard on Emma.

"I mean, I might just have her sold, by the time we are supposed to leave Casablanca and I'd go back alone!"

She turned on a sweet tone and where Emma was unpacking in her suitcase.

"Shall we go to the traditional "Tomatina Festival later, today?"

"Nya, don't feel like looking at a bunch of red stained tomato people and that while dodging, missing being pelted, with same!"

"So what do you feel like doing, I'm free for the rest of the day. Do something with your mommy?" She teased.

"I'll do some catching up of reading, I'll be okay!"

Mary lost her temper now and in anger, retorted.

"You just want to be alone and think of Anton and home. You are just a spoilt brat. Your father spoiled you rotten and you have no ambition. Never mind, I will find something for myself to do. Stay. Read your book!"

When Mary spun on her heel and left the room, Emma allowed her eyes to follow Mary and she breathed.

"I've always wondered how she gets it right to spin on her heel and wag her tail, at the same time!"

Emma bounced onto the bed and started paging through a magazine.

Having decided on walking a distance, Mary enjoyed the tree lined boulevards and sat by a sidewalk restaurant, drinking strong black coffee. She giggled once and said.

"I shall have to wear a djellaba, like the Moroccon ladies here wear. But how on earth can one dress with long sleeves and robe extending to the ankles, so as to sidestep the attention of these men that flirt so openly, in public!"

She was sitting quite alone and allowed her thoughts wings, saying.

"The women here try never to walk unaccompanied. I also read that they are brought up from small, to have thick skins and ignore remarks from these delightful, French speaking, men. Be warned they say on the pamphlet, that harassment is unavoidable in Morocco. And I'm not supposed to react? Mmm! And I was just thinking that Gavin was boring me lately, making me feel like a housewife. Yughh!"

Some men walked by now and while staring at Mary made whistling sounds, discussing her among each other, all the while. She smiled back at them as she crossed her well-proportioned legs.

"Don't react, the pamphlet says, how can one not want to break out of all the rules and flirt back?"

"How can a woman alone in a romantic city, resist the charm of such handsome men?" She debated, while smiling coyly.

She also read that crowded conditions at the medinas and souks are the reason for much pilfering and pick pocketing, there. She slipped the pamphlet into her bag and showed with her arm, for a waiter. She ordered another cup of coffee from the charming man who served her. When he placed her cup down, he tried in broken English to ask her.

"I move the table inside?"

"No, I'm happy out her!"

"Mademoiselle!" He started but she insisted that she was happy sitting right where she was and the man disappeared explaining this, while throwing his hands in the air, to the other waiters, who only stared at her.

She had on her time, finished her coffee and before wondering why the streets seemed empty, a nearing noise caught her attention. A crowd filling the tree lined, boulevard came running and she gasped.

"Oh Shit, it's the Tomatina festival!"

Frozen to the small chair by a table on the sidewalk, Mary sat quite still, not knowing where she would be the safest.

"That crowd looks threatening!" She moaned and held onto the small table. The crowd was upon her and were throwing tomatoes by the baskets full. Mary was in the middle of the whole traditional experience, as tons and tons of very ripe tomatoes flew against her and past her, everywhere. It was within a few minutes when the crowd had pushed past her, screeching with laughter. The people were covered in red fleshy tomato but as the last of the crowd passed, the chair she had tried so hard to hold onto, toppled and she fell onto the pavement. It was the waiter that served her, that came running to her rescue.

"Mademoiselle, I am sorry!"

Another waiter joined him and they pulled her to

her feet. The second waiter tried with his very clean serving cloth, to wipe at her face. When she looked down, she was covered in tomato.

"How the hell could you not have warned me, what was going to happen?"

"Ah Mademoiselle!" He tried to explain but she was shouting now.

"The least you could have done is explain to me, what is going on and that I'm going to be caught in the middle of the procession!"

She stopped and waited for his answer. He started but the second waiter explained.

"We thought you, as a tourist wanted to partake in the procession!"

Her eyes had taken on a deeper green as they do when she becomes so angry.

The first waiter started.

"Mademoiselle, I beg your pardon for what happened and as the Owner of this restaurant I would like to make it up to you, by inviting you in, so you can freshen up and enjoy a glass of French Champagne, with me?"

Astounded now at his reaction, she turned to her humble self-personality and smiled glamorously beneath the layer of tomato pulp, she now wore. He went on.

"My suite is upstairs and be my guest to use the bathroom. I can also send your clothes to cleaners, while you bath!"

"Thank you!" She soothed and followed him upstairs.

"Oh heck, he is scrumptious!" She whispered over and over while lying in the privacy of his bath.

When he came back into the room, she apologized.

"I saw your toweling gown and was tempted while I wait, to wear it, while I read your magazine!"

She stopped but went on when she saw the pleasing look on his face.

"And your bed looked tempting, so I used it, to lay on!"

He gave a warm bursting laugh from his soul, lay her clothing down and when the private suit dining room door opened, he commanded without leaving the room.

"Leave the tray there, thanks!"

He left the room and prepared the trolley with food onto the glass table before he poured the champagne. When she appeared dressed and ready to go, she was taken aback. He stood beside the chair of the table laid out with sliced meats, dried figs, couscous, breads and cheese. The champagne had been poured into long stemmed glasses and when he held her glass out to her, she breathed.

"Oh my gosh, this is a total surprise!"

"I do not know how to make up for the misunderstanding of earlier but if you will allow me the opportunity, I will try!"

"Oh my gosh, we haven't even introduced ourselves yet, I am Mary Ross, business women from the island. Actually I own the island!"

He took her ring finger, saw she wore no ring and kissed it, while holding it to his skin, he said.

"I am Hashim, simple man with restaurant but at your service as long as you may need me!"

Giggling at the circumstance that played out, neither Gavin nor Kevin were anywhere in her thoughts. She had in any case decided that with being one of the richest woman in the world, she deserved to live this life style. She lay back with laughter, enjoying the attention from such a handsome and desirable man, saying.

"It is such an honor to meet you Hashim, I hope we are going to enjoy a wonderful friendship!"

He kissed her hands and then with his gaze, held her eyes. His lips moved up her arm and at her neck, kissed her, sending chills down her spine and she was speechless. He pulled the chair out and allowed her to be seated. They spoke of their lives and being unattached, the loneliness of it. They discussed partners that have jilted them, as if having been rejected. They shed a tear at the hurt of the rejection. And Mary knew this young man, fitted her life, like a glove and she wanted to be with him from now on and experience the love, the innocence, she found in his eyes. Mary was smitten and was not afraid to show it. It seemed he felt the same way and when he pulled her to the bedroom, she did not care for business or money coming in, and in fact Emma was now the last thing on her mind. He was passionate and played her like a fiddler that loved the violin and Mary did not care to ever go back to Gavin. Hashim and Mary stayed in bed for the afternoon. Time had stood still for them, where they stood on the crest of eternity. When she dressed to go, he begged her to stay, saying.

"My Manager will take care of the restaurant and you and I can get to know each other!"

"Two bottles of champagne and an afternoon of

making love with you, I'd say I'd want to stay forever!"

He pulled her back onto the bed and started kissing her.

"I have to go see if my daughter, Emma is okay!"

He moaned and said.

"I shall miss you, but wait for your return!"

While blowing an unseen kiss, Mary took a taxi home, saying to herself when in the backseat and on her way.

"My legs would never have made even walking a block, after that episode!" She giggled and when arriving in the hotel suit, Emma demanded.

"Where were you, I have been phoning you all afternoon?"

"Who died and made you my mother?"

"Mom, I have been worried sick about you!"

Mary's face was radiant, when she announced.

"Oh Emma, I've fallen deeply in love!"

"Mom you're a married woman!"

"I've got to have this man, he speaks French and can offer me a life!"

While holding out her hands as if to shut out her

mother, Emma stated in finality.

"You know what, I don't want to hear it. When are you going to grow up Mother?"

"Just meet him, you'll see what I mean?"

"Please Ems, just meet him?"

"Mom, you make me so angry. All right, but just this once!"

Meeting almost too often while here in Casablanca, Hashim and Mary were both in love and walked hand in hand, wherever they could. He placed his arms around her, more often than not. The waiters at the restaurant, knew her by name and treated her like royalty. Mary was elated, except when she had to tear herself away from Hashim, to see clients, her presentations were not as powerful, as she had been in her life.

"Ems, tonight you're going to meet the man I love with my being, please don't talk of your father, for this evening?"

And when at the restaurant, Hashim had kept the restaurant closed and only for his use, tonight. The place was lit only by millions of candles and when Mary introduced Hashim to Emma, he held onto her hand, taking it between his and looking into her eyes. Emma was impressed by the man and watched her mother like a hawk. It was very late evening, when Mary made her way to the bathroom and Emma and Hashim were alone.

Emma felt slightly uncomfortable and when he stated.

"I'll go look where your Mom is, she has been gone too long now!"

When he came back, he said.

"She's freshening up!"

He showed with his hands to his hair and face and added with a grin.

"Will be here soon!"

It was on walking past Emma, that she felt his gentle touch on her, pulling her from her seat. Emma did not want to be rude and gave a slight giggle. When she stood up, he held her from the back and in her neck, his hot breath, whispered.

"Emma, you are everything a man could want in a women. Please let me be your man, I could look after you, treasure you!"

He spun her around, holding her wrists in one hand now while he pushed her against the wall, kissing her passionately. Whispering all the while, begging her to be his.

The door burst open and Mary stood staring at him, she held a knife in her hand, amplifying.

"I was watching you on the screen, on the

monitor in the bedroom. That is an innocent child, my child. You promised me your love and now?”

Emma shouted now.

“Mom it is not worth stabbing him, killing him, you’ll get into trouble!”

The warning fell on deaf ears as Mary lunged forward and had already stabbed him into his chest and then over and over. The blood spattered onto her face and clothing, even on her hands but she did not stop. Emma was hysterical, begging for her to stop, but only when Hashim fell to the floor and let out his last breath, did she stop and stare at what she had done.

“Let’s get out of here, Emma!”

Through her tears Emma, amplified.

“You’re full of blood, let me wipe you off first?”

“Don’t touch anything, don’t want to leave fingerprints!”

Calm now, Mary kept staring at him, saying.

“And I thought this was love!”

Not being able to utter a word, Emma used a roll of toilet paper and cleaned her mother off, while placing the soiled paper into a plastic bag and taking it with them when they left. They left through a back entrance. The restaurant had long closed and Mary used tissue on her fingers to unlock the kitchen door, shutting it behind them. They walked the small way back to their hotel.

In the lobby of their hotel, Mary greeted the staff and Emma wondered.

"How can Mom be so calm, after what just happened?"

In the suite, Mary waited till she had bathed and the clothing she had worn was knotted up safely in a plastic bag and thrown away into the containers, behind the hotel.

Mary spoke first in their walk back to their suite from the containers.

"No one will recognize me as the one who killed Hashim, I touched nothing and the clothes and shoes are all gone. Tomorrow after my interview with the client, I will go to Hashim's Restaurant and pretend I'm looking for him, not knowing that he is dead!"

While staring at her mother, Emma's heart broke to see her this way.

"She is probably in shock!"

When Mary arrived at Hashim's Restaurant, she smiled, confident that they knew not, who killed Hashim.

She asked for the man she loved and was

ushered into the office area, by the manager, who explained.

"Till what time did you visit with Hashim last night?"

"Around Seven!" She answered with a worried frown, pretending to prepare herself for the shock.

He spoke.

"Mademoiselle, we have had very bad news. Hashim was stabbed with a knife last night at around 12:00. Do you recall anyone else being here, before you left?"

Her hands automatically went up over her mouth and she asked.

"Is he okay?"

"The police say, they think when you left, another person must have come in to see him!"

"Is he okay?" Mary asked, while standing up now.

"Sorry Mademoiselle but he passed away!"

Her cries were heard into the restaurant. Mary was overwrought by everything that had happened and now let the held back shock and disappointment, have their way.

On confiding in Emma, Mary gave a small laugh and said.

"I think I have thrown the police off my trail!"

On staring at the woman she had always called Mom, Emma admitted to herself.

"What's wrong with her, Dad always stood as a buffer, protecting us from her sharp tongue, but this?"

And she shook her head.

After the incident with Hashim, Mary when being accosted by men, would draw her top lip up to her nose and make a face at their charm.

"That would keep you from flirting that easily!"

And they would turn away, leaving her to be.

"Not going to go through that again!" She breathed while sauntering with Emma beside her through the handcrafts at the Mohammed V Square, which lay almost behind the Hassan II Mosque

"Oh Emma look at these Persian carpets and the leather craft!"

Her daughter stayed at her side now like a body guard, watching her mother's every move.

Emma put in.

"Oh gosh, look at the jewelry!"

Something had changed inside of Mary in the way that she did not want to open herself to men that she did not know and so she was able to resist the charm of the Moroccan men that in their outspoken way, charmed many a women.

It was neither Emma nor Mary that noticed when doing sight-seeing that they were being followed. Mary was saying to Emma.

"I have always wanted to see what the Catholic Church looks like inside and now I have the opportunity!"

While alighting the stairs, she turned to Emma asking.

"Did you know that they are the richest Church in the world?"

Emma shook her head and Mary in excited tone went on to say.

"This is the Cathedrale Sacre Coeur or the Casablanca Cathedral!"

"Oh my gosh, look at the magnificence of the architecture!"

Once having reached the top step, it was but a few meters to entering through the heavy wooden doors into a reception area and directly in the church. The red carpets absorbed their movement and once into the church you could but hold your breath at not wanting to break the awesomeness of the moment. The windows were mosaic glass and as the sun shone onto these, the brilliance of the artist came alive showing the crucifixion of Jesus. Mary broke the intense silence by whispering and holding onto Emma's arm.

"Oh my gosh, I don't have words. It's nothing like I imagined!"

"Shht. Mom!"

But she carried on to say.

"Look at the Holy statues of the Mother Mary, Joseph the Carpenter, Oh my gosh this is too overwhelming. Where do you think, we could buy some of this art work?"

On staring at Mary long and hard, Mary turned to Emma asking.

"What?"

"What do you want to do with the statues?"

"Have them in our home, I'm sure they are collector pieces. Could be worth a fortune!"

"Oh my hat. Where did I get a mother like you?"

They were standing now in front of the alter at the kneeling pew. Mary knelt down, while placing a loose lying pillow beneath her knees. Emma stared at her while hiding her face. A few nuns entered the church and kneeled beside Mary. Emma made her way, fleeing the embarrassment of her mother and sat in the congregation benches, waiting for her. The Nun's made the sign of the cross on kneeling and Mary also did the same before she pinched her eyes closed and held her hands at her mouth, folded in prayer. While searching in her bag Emma found a mint and sucked at this while taking in the every move of Mary. The Nun's left and when Mary turned to Emma, she showed for her to join her. Emma walked a small way toward her, when Kevin stood suddenly beside her.

"Emma I'm here to fetch you back, your mother is a very sick person and I want you to trust me, to keep you safe!"

Mary jumped up from her knees, but Kevin had already put the fingers of his one hand around her neck and was gripping her tightly while demanding.

"You have killed, stolen and destroyed. I'm taking you in for arrest!"

"Dad, don't hurt her, she is not well, is doing strange stuff!"

"Sit there Emma!" He demanded and pulled Mary behind the marble tabernacle, throwing her to the floor with the pistol pointed into her back. A few Nuns came in to morning-prayer. They smiled lovingly at Emma, not knowing that behind the

Tabernacle, lay Mary with Kevin while he was pushing her face into the floor and holding the pistol pointing at her. Hardly had the voices left when he pulled her by her neck into a standing position. Mary was shaking while Kevin had never in his life, felt such hatred for anyone. It was when Kevin pulled her by the hair toward Emma that Mary grabbed the pure gold candlestick and beat him through his face. When he for the moment let her go, she grabbed Emma, saying to her.

"I'll take you at gunpoint Emma, if I have to!" She demanded this while reaching for the pistol in her bag.

In the running Emma, even while being out of breath, spoke.

"Mom, you're not well. We have to get to a doctor!"

"What is wrong with me?"

"Stress Mom, I heard it plays havoc on the human!"

"Man, there is nothing wrong with me!"

They fled and when safely in their suite and while lying on her bed, Emma brought her some tea.

"Thanks!" She said sipping it slowly.

"Mom, would you honestly shoot me?" Emma asked curious.

"Oh, it's just that I don't ever want to be without you, Emma!"
"Oh!"

Kevin's face was bleeding badly and as Mary and Emma had disappeared, he left back to his hotel suite. Rick accused.
"Where the hell did you get beaten up?" I thought we decided that we will stick together!"
"While you were still sleeping, I decided to take a walk down the road to the bazaars. Was just going to sight see for a while but then I saw Mary and Emma and I followed them. She hit me with a gold candlestick in the face!"
Rick shook his head.
"That woman does nothing cheap!"
He thought for a moment, before asking.
"Where did she get the gold candlestick from?"
"We were in the Catholic Church!"
Rick thought hard but then asked.
"You could not wait for her to get out of church before starting the fight, could you?"
Kevin tried not moving his lips when laughing but said.
"You're sounding too much like a wife lately, Rick!"

As soon as Kevin's face was healed slightly, he and Rick started their search for Mary who had decided to stay indoors in the romantic city of Casablanca. Mary ran her office from inside the suit, on the top landing of the hotel, which overlooked a city of modern day skyscrapers and cobble streets down into the tree lined boulevards. It was when Emma insisted to leave the suite that Mary lost her temper, shouting.

"You are putting both our lives in danger. Your father will kill us!"

"Mom, why would dad kill us, what have you done?"

"He's off his head. You saw him at the church. I was only sitting praying and look what he did to me!"

Emma could not help but laugh at her mother, while knowing in her heart.

"Dad will never kill me!"

It was late one night and Emma was already asleep in her hotel suite when there was a noise and she knew it was not Mary. Her heart was beating wildly.

"It sounds like footsteps on the thick carpet!" She sounded.

It was sudden and two men stood at her bedside in the moonlight. She was sitting upright.

"We're not going to hurt you, Emma but just come with us and don't make a sound!"

Afraid now at the balaclava men, she put her gown and slippers on and followed them. They walked up to the top landing where the helipad was and Emma was told to get into the waiting helicopter. Hardly was she inside, when Mary, while carrying the briefcase arrived, escorted by two strong men. They threw her into the helicopter and once the helicopter had taken off, they asked Mary.

"Are you going to keep your mouth shut, or must we leave the tape covering it on!"

Mary was crying now and when they ripped the tape off, she held her mouth for a moment. She and Emma sat side by side and behind them were two guards, in front of them were another two. Mary asked.

"Where are you taking us?"

"To Paris, Madame!"

"Why, I finished doing business there!"

The guard in the front gave a snort and acknowledged.

"No. You did not finish business with us. Your

husband killed our two men that were fetching the Serum, so now we shall again, get the original from you!"

He threw his head back and added.

"This time free!"

The helicopter landed at the airfield, where a private plane was already waiting. One of the men turned to Emma and while placing his hand on her knee said.

"My darling and you need not be afraid, we are not going to hurt you or the first "Brilliant" as your mother calls your baby. We are enthusiastic to own, such a discovery of a human being!"

The plane ride to France was comfortable even having a place to rest for Emma. She was given a glass of Cola and some biscuits and left to rest.

Mary was resting in the chair. She looked calm but inside of her, her mind was racing. It was when crossing Toulon that the aircraft suddenly started shaking. Knowing that something was wrong, Emma and Mary immediately fastened their seatbelts, knowing that something was amiss.

"Mom I'm scared!" Emma said.

"Don't worry Emma, the pilots are probably of the very best!" Not sounding very convincing, Mary answered nervously. Emma couldn't hide the fear in her voice, sensing that Mary was not being truthful and she asked.

"Mom, are you sure they're experienced as they never even gave the order of fastening our seatbelts?"

Mary did not answer. From where she was sitting, Mary sensed tension taking place in the pilots' cabin. When one of the men came by, she asked.

"What is wrong?"

"Engine trouble!"

She could hear by the screeching sound that came from one of the engines, that there were problems. Mary thought of Gavin and wondered why she was not like other women that would have given her all, to stay home and be safe as an ordinary housewife. The plane seemed to be pulling to one side, even causing her to be nauseous, but she stayed where she was, keeping a watch on the room door, where Emma was having a nap.

"I'll kill anyone that touches her!" She whispered.

The plane was losing altitude, Mary could feel the nose of the plane tipping. Meanwhile in the cockpit, there was much arguing going on and when two of the men shouted at Emma.

"Get to your seat!" She fell into the seat next to Mary, she asked.

"What's going on?"

"Engine trouble!" Mary stated flatly.

Mary turned to see where the men walking by were going but Emma asked.

"What are they going to do now?"

"I don't know!" Mary shrugged.

A terrible vacuum sucking sound came from the door.

"Stay her Emma, keep your seat belt on!"

She made her way to the door, pushing it with all her might, before she shouted.

"Help me Emma, they have opened the door to get out?"

When the sucking noise settled, Mary demanded.

"I'm going to the cockpit follow me, but be careful!"

The seats in the cockpit were empty.

"There's no one flying the plane!" Mary blurted out.

"Bastards! All of them, they left us and parachuted out!"

She also added.

"I didn't trust their arrogance.

Seated in the pilots chair now she, put the

speaker to her mouth just as Emma fell into the chair, next to her.

"Hello!" Mary said into the mouthpiece, praying that someone would hear her. Her voice was shaking and she gave a sigh of relief when a voice sounded.

 "What is your position?"

In a small voice Mary while trying to make some sense out of the control panel before her, spoke.

"I don't know!"

"Can you see the GPS?" He asked.

Mary scanned the panel and read their position from the GPS.

"I've got that!" The man replied continuing calmly.

"I have just picked you up on our radar screen and I see that you're losing altitude. Please fasten your seat belts and take hold of the steering column. Can you spot the fuel gage on your left hand side? Wait, which side are you sitting on Mademoiselle?"

"Right hand side!" Mary shouted through the mouth piece but she carried on.

"Tell me what to do?" She did not give him a chance but carried on to say.

"The engines are making strange sounds and you better help me to get this plane onto the ground!"

Again demanding she screamed.

"Tell me what to do. The engines are making strange sounds and you had better help me get this plane onto the ground!"

It was within a moment that she started to cry.

"I can feel the plane going down!"

"Ma'am calm down, I've got your position!"

"What must I do with the steering column? I've seen on the movies that I must pull it back towards me!"

"Yes, put both hands on the column and pull back ever so slightly back and see that your plane's speed picks up!"

Mary was pulling the column towards her and the plane's nose lifted towards the sky. She smiled with relief and thought.

"Well done Mary Ross, you can fly!"

But her joy was short lived, because as the nose lifted, the plane went up too fast and slowed down.

The controller asked.

"Where is the pilot and what is your name, please?"

"The pilot and his cronies, parachuted out and left my daughter and me!"

"My name is Mary Ross!"

A few seconds of silence followed before he exclaimed.

"Oh Shit, you are going to try and follow my instructions! My name is Jacques!"

"Okay! Jacques, the plane just started nose diving again.   I think I did something wrong with the steering column!"

"Do you see the gauges directly to your left?"

Mary looked.

"Yes I do, I see two gauges but forget the gauges and tell me how to fly. Mary demanded nervously as she added.

"It feels as though my lungs are bursting from not breathing..

"Do you see them? Can you read them?"

 "Now lady, you are going to have to do some steering, as you would call it, when driving a car. Now take hold of the steering wheel of the car. Can you pull it slightly, very slightly up?"

A silence reigned. In fear, Mary shouted.

"You're an air traffic controller and you're telling me I'm driving a car?"

Mary was beside herself with fear and rage, even towards Jacques who was telling her what to do.

"I'm Mary Ross, no one tells me what to do and in that tone of voice!"

"Jacques, listen!" She started.

The plane was going down and she suddenly remember that she was going down with it.

"Jacques, listen!"

But the plane accelerated suddenly and she shouted.

"I'm pulling it close to me but!"

She gave it another moment before she said.

"But the nose of the plane is not turning up!"

"Try again Ma'am, try lifting the steering column, and pull it down towards your tummy!"

"I can't, I can't!"

"Emma!" She was screaming but suddenly slumped forward.

On entering the cockpit, Emma summed up the situation and sat down beside her mom.

"She's fainted!" Emma breathed.

Emma fastened her seatbelt and put on the head piece, saying.

"This is Emma speaking!"

There was a short and uneasy silence, Jacques said in a calm and controlled voice.

"Mary…Emma??

"Mary passed out, I'm her daughter. Tell me what to do!"

"Take the steering column and pull it slowly

towards you!”

“I am pulling the steering column and the plane definitely does not budge. By looking at the gauges, I see that the one engine is not working at all and the second one is busy going!”

“Well Emma you are doing a mighty fine job but I now want you to switch the engines both off, you are flying very low!”

“Do you see the blue and red lever to the right? Pull both out and then push them back again, as soon as the engines have stopped!” Jacques instructed.

“They are both switched off now!”

“Well, try starting the plane once again. Push them in again!”

Before he could explain he heard the whining of the plane engine but she reported.

“It did not start but I’m going to try once again. I presume it’s the start on/off switch?” Emma asked.

“Brilliant, Emma. Do so!” Jacques acknowledged.

It was at that moment that both engines started and when she pulled the steering column, the nose of the plane rose.

She reported this and he answered.

“Very well, Emma, now Emma you are flying

rather low and you are flying very fast. The lever next to your seat, pull it back slowly. When the plane is level, keep the steering column right there. Look for an opening between the trees and steer the plane ever so slightly, towards the opening. Can you see somewhere you can land?

"Yes, it's right in front of me, the opening between the trees is right in front of me!" Emma breathed this with joy sounding in her voice.

"Great, now pull the lever next to your seat as far back as possible!"

"Done!" Emma replied.

"Your speed looks good. You're nearly there!" Jacques tried hard to sound positive. He continued.

"There is a lever with a white top to your right. Pull it down as far as you can!"

Emma threw a quick glance at the flaps that moved and said.

"Flaps down!"

"Brilliant, Emma!" Jacques answered and added.

"I want you to keep the plane steady and in a horizontal position until landing, alright?"

The silence that reigned assured Jacques that the plane was plowing through the trees. Emma did not answer but focused on what she remembered

Uncle Gavin doing. It was within ten minutes that she called into the microphone.

"I think we have landed!"

There was no reply from Jacques, leaving Emma to think that the radio was damaged. She turned toward Mary who was slumped in her seat. Emma smiled for the reason that the crash was over and it went well, better than expected. She started to laugh and to cry at the same time, reliving again the feeling as the plane went crashing through the trees and she was pinching her eyes closed, She was holding her stomach when her hands were free as to protect the baby while the plane struck tree after tree, until it slowed down. In the quiet of the moment all she could see before her was Anton's smile and she could feel his arms around her. She was calm. The image of the waterfall appeared calling her through, bringing her peace.

"Why does this warm and wonderful feeling come across me when I see this waterfall?" She wondered.

And when this feeling left her, she saw Anton before her, smiling and holding out his hands. She opened her eyes slowly and before her a few feet away, she knew that the plane was dangling from the trees.

"Hallo!" Emma spoke into the microphone, trying to see if she could talk to Jacques.

Great relief flooded over her when his voice came.

"Emma. Are you okay? And Mary?" Jacques asked slowly. He was sitting on the edge of his seat and for the first time as an air traffic controller, he experienced doing a crash landing. He spoke.

"You have just survived a crash landing!"

He also asked.

"Now Emma, are your engines off?"

"No engines!" She spoke softly, repeating.

"Engines gone!"

No other words left her lips but she formed her lips saying.

"They're gone!"

At that moment the plane began to sway and tilt, sliding down into the forest of trees, where it had landed.

Emma screamed when the plane dived towards the ground. Glancing at Mary, she realized that her mother was coming to.

"Thanks mom for your support!" Emma in sarcastic tone, blurted out also informing.

"What a day and you passed out!"

"Emma?" Jacques sounded.

But at the same time a loud crack came when the branches beneath the plane snapped and tore. The plane slid down in among them. It only stopped when the nose hit the ground and the tail was resting against stems of mature trees.

"We're going to be okay!" Emma breathed.

 Jacques talked quickly, his voice started to grow softer and softer. Emma knew the radio was going to die in a few seconds and she listened.

The last she heard from Jacques was.

"Emma if we lose contact, I want you to know that we have your position pinpointed and I want you to stay for a while as far from the plane as possible, in case of fire. But we need you to be close enough to the plane, so we can find you, when we arrive with help!"

The sound disappeared. Emma switched off the intercom and turned to Mary, whispering.

"She must have bumped her head, when we slipped from the trees!"

"Mom, mom, it's okay, were safe, let's get out of here?"

Emma helped her to the entrance of the plane.

All sound had disappeared, leaving them also in total darkness and she whispered.

"Mom are you all right?"

Sobbing now, Mary pleaded.

"How are they going to find us, if were in a thicket of trees, where we cannot be spotted from the air?"

"Mom, you have to be strong now. We have to get away from the plane in case of fire, I'm taking the blankets, hold onto my hand, we have to get out of here!"

Emma looked from the planes ripped door, to the ground and bravely said.

"I'm going to clamber to the bottom and bunch the blankets for you to fall onto!"

On climbing down against a tree, Emma turned back to see Mary staring down at the ground below. Emma spoke harshly to her mother now.

"Mother take a hold of yourself. You have to do this and hurry, in case of fire!"

Now sitting on the side of the plane's doorway, Mary wiggled herself over, to a position where she was able to reach out for the broken tree branches. And Mary threw down the briefcase first. And then while hanging in midair, her feet searched for a place to grip, giving the weight on her arms relief.

It was on looking back in the moonlight that

Emma landed and called.

"See Mom, it was not so difficult!"

Emma looked back to see Mary holding onto branches and making her way down. Mary's arm muscles felt as though they were tearing from her body but while making a swinging movement, she moved her body down the tree. Lower down on the tree stem and out of view from the plane opening, it became darker and when on the ground, Emma had already placed the Eiderdowns, hoping to soften the fall, for Mary.

"Mom what were you thinking throwing that briefcase down, it could have killed me?"

"Our future Emma, were going to live it in style, if I can help it!"

That statement brought Mary back to reality for the moment and she remembered how she had clambered this distance, from the helicopter. And she in the moonlight, looked down and saw the pile of blankets and while pulling her skirt up to her waist, aimed and bounced into them.

"Oh my gosh. Mother you were not supposed to jump, we cannot afford to sprain an ankle now!"

The moon appeared reaching into the forest of trees, Mary stood up, grabbed the briefcase and while gathering the blankets, took Emma's hand, exclaiming.

"We're alive and no fire is going to take that from us now, run Emma!"

Holding onto her stomach as if to cradle the baby with one hand, Emma ran and when at a safe distance, Emma threw the blankets down, spreading these for herself and for Mary. While still giggling the two lay down. Emma held onto the woman that had been her mother for as long as she could remember. They spoke of the stars that winked through the openings, as the wind moved through the trees. They spoke of the owl that hooted up high and the crickets that sounded close and when they fell asleep, Emma wondered.

"Will you forget me Anton and what of baby? Will we ever see each other again? And how much chance, will baby have of survival if my life is in such a mess?"

In the moonlight Emma stared at her mother. Where she lay on the blanket, she had fallen into a deep sleep. Now, pulling the briefcase closer, Emma while throwing another glance at her mother, softly opened the locks and stared at the contents.

"Cash, cheques, money, eee, pistol, hard drive all

wrapped up, and bags of medication!"

Not being able to sleep, Emma listened to the sounds of the night.

"Like Uncle Gavin did and loved!"

She listened to the rustle of leaves that lay on the ground, listening for footsteps. She listened for the motor engine of an overhead plane and she lay with fear and listened for the sound of fire from the engine of the plane that had brought them and been abandoned. Leaving Emma and Mary to their own fate, for the French men steering the plane, was easier than risking their lives further after having captured the women.

Turning to Mary, Emma put her arms around the woman who birthed her and held her till morning light. It was Mary that woke first, saying.

"Let's get to the plane, I'm hungry!"

And when back at the place of landing, Mary asked while holding her hands to her mouth.

"Oh Gosh, Emma how the hell did you do it?"

Staring at the plane that had slipped into the trees, nose first with its body resting against stems of forest trees, Emma shook her head slowly.

"I don't know mother, I don't know!"

Walking a small distance from where Emma was, Mary suddenly screamed and came running back.

"What's wrong?"

"Oh Emma, I just encountered the ugliest, longest, blackest snake that I have ever seen. It got a fright at my movement and crawled into the hole right where he was lying. Emma had her arms around Mary while Mary was explaining.

"Emma it was at least a meter long!"

"We'll just have to keep a look out and be careful!"

A plane sounded, circling above but eventually disappeared. By late afternoon, Mary was crying.

"I honestly cannot sleep out here, knowing that snake is around, in any case, I'm famished!"

"Let us in some way try and get up into the safety of the plane?"

"Oh, heck I do hope that thing does not slide down with us in it?"

"At least were away from snakes and whatever else predator here may be!"

Measuring the distance they had to get up against the tree, Emma stated.

"I'll help you up Mom. Get into the tree and as close as the opening of the plane, just get inside!"

"Emma, the baby, just be careful!"

There was a chill in the air and Emma was thankful that tonight would not be spent down in the forest. It took some climbing for Emma to get herself and her mother into the plane. Once inside, it was not easy to do anything with the plane being upright, but Emma even found a fridge with cool drinks and food and biscuits and some breads. She ripped the mattress from the bed where she had lay after being kidnapped and while placing it onto the now upright, cockpit wall, they lay flat on their backs, and while eating and drinking giggled at the experience they had come through with only scratches on their arms and legs.

"I don't know when, I tell him or her about it when he or she turns 21 someday, how this baby is going to cope with all the action of these past 24 hours!"

They giggled like sisters and Emma loved her mother, in spite of her weird ways. It was then when Emma remembered the radio and in some manner, tried to reach the airfield. When she returned to where Mary lay, Emma stated.

"They can't hear me!"

Another night was spent in the darkness in the

middle of no-where, but this time at least in the safety away from the snake. On opening their eyes, at first light of the morning, there was a helicopter circling above. The forest was thick and Emma wondered how to show them exactly where she and Mary were waiting. In reaction to this sound, Mary had started crying and Emma now, held her close. Tears started down her own cheeks but she assured.

"Mom, they will find us, you will see!"

Wondering to herself, Emma thought.

"Mom what have you done to your life and how the heck are you going to get out of this mess?"

It was on hearing the scrunching of twigs beneath someone's feet that they heard the voice.

"I've found the plane!" And he gave directions.

Crawling along the wall of the plane to the opening Emma popped her head out.

"Are you Emma?" He asked.

She nodded.

"We have you and you need not be afraid anymore. We've come to save you and your mother. The team will be here right now!"

It was a relief to not have to climb down the tree stems again as many strong hands held onto Emma and baby and lifted them to safety. Mary stayed quiet through the whole ordeal and Emma was thankful. A helicopter was waiting and they were taken back to their hotel in Casablanca.

The person responsible for finding Mary and Emma this time was Philip when he reported of the kidnapping and plane crash, where in Mary and Emma were saved.

"The Rescue team was not aware of Mary's tricks or she would have been arrested but that I want to have the pleasure of doing myself. They are back in the Marrakesh hotel and I have men onto them!"

It was Rick that confided.

"I am now heartily sick and tired of running like a puppet after the woman, let's take her in. We spike the drinks, chloroform the guards and take your daughter firstly, give Mary over and get out of here. "Cannot take this cat and mouse game anymore!"

Being dressed as waiters did help some as Mary on the receiving end did not care who did the giving. She received the champagne and chocolates with the get well card, with open arms as if to deserve such. She did not drink it.

Kevin who had injected medication into the fruity light alcohol drink, was sure that Emma would not have any. Sitting back in the privacy of her suite, while enjoying a long stemmed glass of the fruit nectar, Mary phoned client after client, just to wish them a wonderful weekend but introduced her "Brilliant" offer at the same time. It was the last thing on her mind that Rick on behalf of Kevin, would make contact with Emma.

It was in surprise when she opened her suite door.

"Uncle Rick it is so nice seeing you. My mom is in her suite busy doing business, come in for a while, please. Tell me how my Dad is doing?"

"Emma that is why I am here, your father wants to help you get out of this mess. He wants you and your baby safely home!"

"Uncle Rick!" She started and wondered how to explain to him.

"Firstly, I have fallen in love with Anton but will definitely be coming to visit Dad but at a later stage. Uncle Rick, this is only for Dad to know. Mom is not well and I feel I have to protect her until she can get help. I won't leave her till then!"

Rick left disappointed and did not know how to explain this to Kevin.

It was the following day when Rick again came with a message from Kevin. Oblivious of Rick and his visit, Mary was preparing for three clients saying.

"I have three high bids. Nothing stops me from taking one higher than that of the Sheik, actually wish it were triplets that Emma was carrying!"

Later in finality Mary claimed.

"Now to decide which one would be able to offer me the most secure deal and Emma and the "Brilliant" will have the best life, one could wish for, a mother and child.

Mary was still in conference with the clients when security let her know that.

"A man is with Emma and we are not sure what you, Miss Mary wants us to do, seeing that you, Miss Mary, did not let us know that a visitor is going to be coming around!"

She went to the security room and stared at the screen.

"Oh please, that is Rick. He is spying for the ex-Mr. Ross. Please take care of him for me?"

And she turned at peace that she, Mary, will.

"I'll get my power back and wipe the whole lot

out!"

While in the presence of Emma, Rick was removed by three men and taken to the back office where illegal dealings normally took place. Philip had his men as usual, follow Kevin and Rick.

"Just to keep a hand on what they too were getting up to with Mary being as free as a bird!"

It was when the back room of the office for illegal dealings, door closed that Philip's men decided, seeing that Mary, was in a conference, it was time to see what was up with Rick and when the locked door would not open, one of them pulled a gun with a silencer on, out and fired at the lock. The thud sound was hardly noticed but the men who kidnapped Rick, were holding him in front of the 9th storey window and were about to open it and throw the evidence of him having been there over, the balcony. When the door opened, four of Philips heavily armed men, burst in. The scene played out soundlessly. To the surprise of the men planning to throw Rick into the streets below, Philips men roughly pulled Rick away from them and left while not saying a word. The men inside the office looked at each other and in French spoke.

"What the hell happened there?"
On reporting this incident, Mary lost her deals and was swiftly taken by private plane during the night for Switzerland. Sitting by her side Emma was elated.

It was when Emma and Anton were sitting in the living room, on the sofa, that she suddenly fell over backwards and shouted.
"Oww!"
"What's that my love?" Anton asked dismayed at the urgency of her cry.
"I had a terrible pain in my lower abdomen!"
When walking into the room, Gavin asked.
"What's up?"
"Emma is having terrible pain!"
Now rushing into the room, Mary asked.
"Where are you having pain, Emma?"
Emma showed with her hand below her naval.
"It subsides, but comes back again.
While placing her hand on Emma's stomach, Mary informed.
"The baby's early. We had better arrange with the hospital that we are on our way so they can stand by!"
Staying calm, Gavin instructed Anton.

"Stay with your fiancé, I'll get the helicopter ready and inform the hospital!"

Having disappeared to the bathroom Mary was now scrubbing her hands and saying.

"Round and round against every sound, scrubbing perfecting, don't make mistakes!"

Making Emma comfortable all the time was his up offering as to the pain, she was going through and Anton loved her with his being.

"You, all right, my love?" He kept asking.

When nodding her head at him she would give him a weak smile but he saw more than that, in her. He saw the Emma he had learned to love, the pure and innocent Emma, that allowed him to be her Maestro in life and now she was on the verge of presenting the Maestro with a fruit of their love. When Gavin gave the word that the Helicopter was ready, Anton lifted his wife into his arms, kissing her first and when her arms were safely around his neck, he lifted her carefully, like treasure of a breaking kind. In the helicopter they did not look out to see as the snows had melted, leaving a wonderland of green grasses and short flowers, where fairies and elves play. Gavin while wearing a frown, kept his eyes glued to the instruments of the helicopter and Anton from where he sat in the back gave a running commentary of the well-being of Emma.

It was convenient to land on top of the hospital on their helipad and Anton almost relaxed but remembered that the child birth lay ahead.

He stood at the emergency room curtain, when he heard the sister say. "She's not dilated!"

The sister was smiling when she spoke to him.

"Are you the father?"

"Si, Yes, I'm the father of the child!"

And he fled to the waiting room to where Mary and Gavin were.

Mary had left the waiting room and was busy on her cell phone speaking to the Sheik.

"I'll keep you posted!" She informed and clicked the phone closed.

A mischievous glint played in Gavin's eyes when he noticed the huff Anton was in and Gavin put his hand on Anton's shoulder saying.

"Relax Son, she's in good hands!"

Anton blurted out.

"She's having Braxton Hicks contractions, I do not understand!"

Gavin gave a small laugh saying.

"That's all right, it give us more time for the

baby to stay in the incubator growing and getting stronger!"

Disappointed by the whole situation, Mary explained while biting on her lip.

"The womb is practicing for the birth!"

"Oh!" He answered and again was gone.

The four who were prepared for a birth did not know if they should burst into joyous laughter or be disappointed when taking the journey back home to the Alps.

Trying hard to hide her anger at the false alarm, Mary stared out through the window and did not say much. While steering the helicopter and giving her a glance every now and again, Gavin understood Mary, maybe better than she understood herself. He fussed about Emma and her being so brave. He had even rushed off while all were settled and waiting in the hospital and bought two boxes of fudge and nuts. One from himself and one from Anton.

In Mary's mind, she lulled over.

"How the hell do I tell the Sheik it is a false alarm, I was so sure that he can pay over the money!"

When they arrived home in the Alps, she excused herself, saying.

"I have such a migraine!"

He sat in his favorite chair till late night. The fire in the hearth crackled in the dark and embers shot tiny coals.

"As Emma says, like dancing goblins!"

Gavin closed his eyes and drank in the cries of wolves, which howled at the full moon. He whispered.

"These wolves were brought to Switzerland as an experiment by the Swiss to try and live in the nature reserve set up in the Alps. Gavin was intrigued by their sound. He thought of going there the few times to see them and was awestruck by their eyes, their family system!" And he gave a small laugh.

He was content. Mrs. S. brought in a tray with biscuits and hot chocolate, greeting when she left the room. The house smelled of aniseed rusks, drying in the oven. Far off the loud crack of a pinnacle of ice came, from where it snapped away from the cliff and fell, landing far below allowing the earth to shudder with the impact. He soothed.

"Just mercy!"

Gavin stoked the fire, poured a whiskey and then sat staring into the red of the coals until they were but ash.

In the morning it was Mrs. S. who was first to enter the room.

"I knew you would be sitting here Mr. Gavin. I knew too, after a sleepless night of thinking, cheese grillers and eggs would be welcome!"

She placed down the tray and left.

3 JOHANNESBURG

Looking from the window of the client's plane from up high, one could notice the stream of hot air from its engines, as they embraced the lift-off. The plane cut almost soundlessly through the air. It was Mary, who as always did all the talking. For Emma it was getting harder and harder to leave the love of her life and her new home, behind. It was also hard for her to know what Mary was doing and not being able to show any sign of knowing or any emotion, as to the knowing. The only comfort for Emma was that Anton, the love of her life, was around. She allowed her mind to wander, thinking of the books on pregnancy that she had been reading. She was bored traveling with Mary and debated to herself.

"After reading all the books on pregnancy, the one magazine said that there is an urgent need for the female human being, to make nest for the new chick, before the birth!"

She laughed at her chosen wording but reasoned to herself.

"And for the love of my life, who I am to marry in the summer after the baby is born, it is just getting harder and harder to leave him, even if it is for shopping, as Mom says!"

Chattering on, Mary in excited tone, was telling Emma of the Pilansberg mountain range.

"It runs a fair way, through Southern South Africa!" She carried on though.

"The Resort we will be staying at, has a massive crater on. And that done by some outer space object, hitting the earth, at a speed. It is so deep that when one goes out on their breakfast safari, before the crack of dawn, when standing up high on the hills and mountains, it can be seen from all over the resort!" She waited for Emma to acknowledge the information, before she added.

"It is filled with deep, dark green waters!"

Emma nodded an understanding nod but did not care much to see a crater hole filled with water at this moment of time, she wanted to be home with Anton. And Mary spoke on.

"There is every kind of animal, where you walk in the Resort alone, even lion and cheetah. But they are kept in a giant encampment, where you have to stay in your vehicle or on the open safari vehicle, as this encampment is where these animals roam free!"

There was more excitement in Mary than Emma had seen, in a long time but she just carried on and on.

"So Emma, we will be staying at the Lost City Hotel. It is a hotel being the cream of the crop, snuggled between mountains. The entrance is breathtaking with massive statues of bronzed, life like animals, greeting you, from every corner!" She asked.

"Are you even listening?"

"Yes, Mom, I'm listening to every friggin word!"

"Well, then I need to tell you that there are restaurants and clothing shops, inside. You will love it!”

Staying quiet now Emma carried on lulling her thoughts around but Mary insisted, on going on.

“Do you know when we walk a small way from the hotel there is a bridge. Every short while, a thunderous noise begins and the ground shakes like an earth quake!”

“But listen to this!” Mary insisted while tapping Emma’s arm.

“At the swimming area!” And she stopped, looked if she had Emma’s attention, before she carried on.

“The place is called the Sea of Waves. You must remember they are hours and hours away from the seaside. But here in the middle of nowhere, here between mountains and grass roofed huts, is the Sea of Waves!”

“Sounds impossible mother!”

“Well, huge machines cause movement and the water churns making waves!”

“Sounds spooky to me!”

“Wait you will see. It is apparently awesome!”

Losing interest in her mother’s chattering now, Emma thought of the helicopter ride to meet this plane. Anton was holding her hand when she turned to him and with an almost pleading look, stared at him for a long moment. His heart melted for her and he squeezed her hand, leaned in and kissed her.

"I don't want to go!" She whispered at his lips.

"I want you to go and enjoy the wonderful experience your mother is telling us, of. I don't want you for a moment, to be afraid or not happy!"

Emma wondered how the heck he could be so okay, even to see her go, when she hated it. She wanted to be with him and to her that was all that counted. Half turning, Gavin had asked over his shoulder.

"Are you guys okay?"

Speaking now, Emma disclosed to Gavin.

"Uncle Gavin, I don't want to go with my mother to all the fancy things, she talks about. I want to stay at the cabin!"

He had thrown a glance at Anton, who claimed.

"I've just been telling Emma how amazing Mary has made it sound, she should go and enjoy every minute of the experience, I will be right here, waiting for her!"

Speaking then, Gavin chose his words carefully.

"I think you and the baby need a break from my nagging and from Anton's wining!"

She had burst into laughter and when Anton accused.

"It is Emma that whines, I'm just a happy, chappy!"

Gavin half turned, drank in as she laughed freely before he stated.

"There's my girl. I want to always see you laughing like that!"

She did take the moment to voice her opinion.

"But I really want to stay home!" She started.

And then while losing her temper, Mary had reprimanded.

"Oh Emma, stop it. Just be happy that I take you along!"

She had seen Anton turn his head to stare out of the window, he was wearing a frown and while lifting her hand with the engagement ring on, he put his lips to the ring, kissing it. He then touched her chin gently and said softly.

"It's going to be okay?"

This statement from Anton sent her mind back and reminded her of the previous evening when everyone had already gone to bed. Lying on the couch before the crackling fire, Emma had asked Anton.

"What's on your agenda, till I get back to you?"

"My love, if you ask me rather who is on my mind till you get back, I could answer you and say.

You. You my love. I think of you in my arms and I think of you at my lips. I think of my bride to be and cannot wait for that time to arrive!"

"You make me so happy Anton. I don't know how I am going to live without you, even just for these few days ahead!"

He had leaned over and kissed her lips, saying.

"I will always want the best for you. I want for you to be happy. Now I'm with you and when I'm working, I'm protecting you, I'm working for you, I'm with you. And if someday comes, when I cannot be there for you my love, I will leave you with a sad heart but want you to know, I will support you in finding your happiness because I want you, my love to be happy!"

"What do you mean by that, Anton?"

She sat up right now, staring at him, before she insisted.

"Are you going to leave me?"

"Never. I shall never leave you!"

"Then stop talking nonsense now!"

In broken language he tried to explain, while laughing at the same time.

"I not speak nonsense, you start the nonsense, now you say I speak the nonsense!"

He kissed her frown as if to kiss it away and then while she was still studying his expression, he started tickling her. When she broke out into laughter, he was his happy self and so a beautiful evening of just being together, passed before the fireplace, for Emma and Anton.

While in the helicopter of Gavin earlier, on their way to meeting the plane of Mary's client, Emma had turned to her mother. She held onto Anton's hand and asked.

"I'm old enough to have a baby. Why can I not have freedom of say or what I do?"

Her mother's voice tone had changed, she sounded distant and cold, when she answered.

"We'll talk about that, when settled in the Lost City Hotel!"

Gavin had landed the helicopter and Emma knew not to be humiliated by Mary again, she was not to tarry. On the field, the plane travelling to South Africa was already waiting for them.

Emma had turned back and waved, before she entered the luxury of the private plane. The pilot, wore a broad smile, welcoming them, showing his perfect and milky white, teeth. For the rest of the trip, Emma stared out of the window and Mary was in deep conversation with the client who spoke, saying.

"So were staying over at the Sandton Towers Hotel for a day or two. As you have explained the commission basis of the deal, I have already lined up two clients for us!"

It was with great excitement that Mary broke the news to Emma.

"Oh Emma, we will be staying in the heart of Johannesburg in the Sandton Towers for a day or so while I do business!"

"I heard the first time mom!"

Emma stared at her, asking again.

"When are we going home, Mom?"

"Oh Emma, you will be amazed at the bustle of Johannesburg. I heard it was a mining town, give it a chance. I will put money into your account and you can buy some South African jumpers and clothing, for your little one!"

Being fed up at everything, Emma asked.

"Why do you never call the baby, your grandchild, Mother?"

Mary burst out laughing but immediately stopped, saying.

"Can you picture me as a grandmother,

Emma?”

Staring at her now, Emma waited for her reply.

“Can you imagine me with spectacles and knitting?”

“No, mother, but you can at least pretend!”

Relieved at the landing of the plane, Mary exclaimed.

“Oh, we are already landing, look!”

She also made sure that Emma would not pursue the matter of the child, by saying.

“One hell of a bumpy runway speed, were going at, shit!”

A limousine was waiting and the driver left the partition between the seats open, while Mary spoke, non-stop.

“Oh my word! Look at those mounds along the road. Look Emma, it is as if they glimmer!”

“Ma’am those are gold mines leading into the depths of the earth. They have been mined and as much gold as could be, has been extracted!”

“Do you in Johannesburg have beach sand beneath the ground, the mines are so light in color?”

“The sand has been washed with acid, Ma’am, leaving them to look like beach sand!”

"Is it not dangerous for us to drive here?"

"This is the middle of Johannesburg and those are but the entrances of old shafts, that have been closed and deserted!"

"So there is no chance that these shafts collapse?"

The driver pulled his hat down over his forehead and gave a small laugh, when he said.

"Oh, they do collapse, you can see that they are cordoned off and public are not allowed. But then again Ma'am, it's all a matter of mercy!"

"Oh my goodness!" Mary gasped saying.

"Flyovers and bridges and cars all over to be seen!"

He stopped the car in front of the beautiful white building that reached its architecture, to the heavens and stated.

"Well, here we are Ma'am, the Sandton Towers!"

As if out of nowhere, a porter appeared and helped with the baggage. The driver while smoothing his moustache, adjusted his hat, pulling it to lean far forehead, he reminded in an almost raspy voice.

"The limousine will be at your disposal as long as you stay in South Africa, Ma'am!"

Speaking to Emma now, Mary enthused.

"Do you know how free I feel, to be in a country where I'm not expecting trouble?"

"Actually I love the VIP treatment I get, being with you, Mom!" And she smiled now.

"Well for that, I'm depositing your birthday money with your allowance and I want you to shop, till you drop!"

"Yay, thanks Mom!"

"You won't need to leave the center, if you don't want to. The driver told me that there are plenty of shops, right there!"

Mary invited Emma, let us see the observatory tomorrow?"

Having nodded, Emma knew, Mary would never allow her to get out of the commitment, she had made.

"Interesting dear, all those stars, one feels part of the galaxy!"

Mary carried on though and suggested.

"Let's have lunch?"

"On one condition. Pizza!"

Laughing now, they allowed the driver to choose a suitable place for them.

The following day, Emma was out early. The shops were luxurious and the shoes she saw and fitted, were unique. It was when Emma passed the small bakery and café, inside the building, that she stopped and stared into the fridges, saying.

"Oh my soul. I've got to have that and that!" And she went inside.

Here in the bustle among people, each minding their own business, Emma ate through a custard slice, a big slice of Ganache and a slice of kiwi cheesecake. Feeling utterly sick, she ordered another cup of coffee and then sat there and watched the world go by for a full hour. When she got back to the suit, Mary was sitting in the lounge, painting her toenails. She looked up and asked.

"How was your morning?"

"I'm sick!"

"Judging by all that shopping, I would also be!"

"I'm going to lie down!"

"Emma, I bought you something!"

"What?"

"An evening suit!"

On falling into the chair, Emma moaned.

"Where must I go this time?"

"Were going to a cocktail party, right here in the center, below us!"

"Oh Mom, can't I stay home, please, I'm

pregnant and need rest and I'm homesick!"

"You're always homesick, go lie down and rest, we are leaving at 5, South African time!"

It was at four thirty when Emma came into Mary's suite and announced.

"How do I look?"

"Ravishing, Emma!"

"You look great too Mom, but how come you bought legging suits for both you and I?"

"No reason, just saw yours and thought the powder blue would look good on you with your strawberry blonde hair and for me, the black was slimming and suave!"

Mary stood up from the sofa and demanded.

"Come, let us go!"

The cocktail hall was already filling up with the sound of laughter. A band was playing in the back ground and in the middle of the hall was a table filled with every kind of sliced meat, cold meat, salads, desserts and snacks. Waiters with trays were all over, serving drinks, running back and forth. On beholding what luxury again awaited her, Mary allowed her eyes to drink in a very handsome older man, who was standing among a group. Their eyes met and he almost immediately came over, to where she stood. When Emma saw this, she moved to the back of the room, watching over her mother from afar. A voice from behind Emma spoke into a mobile, saying.

"Yes Mademoiselle. The mother is here and a few minutes ago, she was standing with the daughter. Yes, she is heavily pregnant with the brilliant!"

Frozen for the moment, Emma did not turn but made her way forward to where Mary was throwing her head back at the older man's charm, in laughter. Grabbing now at her mother's wrist, Emma ripped her without a word, saying.

"Come Mother!"

The man at her side, stared in awe and Mary tried to argue with Emma, saying.

"I was just having the most delightful conversation!"

"No time for that Mother, we have to get out of here, right now!"

"But why and let go at my wrist!" Mary demanded.

"Those French guys from the plane, are here!"

"Are you sure?"

"As sure as little green apples, Mom just hurry, we have to get away!"

"I cannot go without my briefcase, Emma!"

Mary thought of the money and the pistol and Emma thought of the tablets and they headed for the suite.

"Got it. Let's get out of here, Emma!"

It was at the lift when Emma noticed that it was slowly nearing their floor. She grabbed at her mother.

"Quick Mom down here!"

When the stairs door shut, while showing with her finger to her lips, Emma pulled her mother, saying.

"Take off your shoes!"

Emma dropped both pairs into the close by waste bin and while still holding onto her mother's wrist, they made their way down the stairs. On throwing the hotel entrance door open, Emma almost bumped into the porter.

"Sorry!" She breathed as they made their way into the streets. Running ahead, Emma stayed pulling her mother along until at a take away hotdog stand, a motor cyclist stopped, he left the bike's engine running. He took a few strides over and ordered meals. On turning around, to keep a watch over his motor bike, he saw Emma push it from its stand and Mary, while clutching the briefcase, climbed onto the back. He shouted but they had already started out of the parking and into the street. Above the noise of the running engine, with Mary hanging onto Emma and the briefcase sticking into Emma's back, the two sped away. It was sudden when Emma turned around, swerving across the road and back the way, they had just come.

"Why are you turning back, Emma? Those men are going to see us?"

"Read the road signs Mother, we have to get to the Pilansberg hotel!"

"The Lost City Hotel, Dear!"

"Same area!" And she carried on to instruct.

"Just help me read the overhead road signs, so we can get there!"

"Where did you learn to drive like this, dear?"

"I've only just learned, Mother!"

When going past the Sandton Towers hotel, Emma saw the two French men dashing from the entrance, into the street. In the running, one still held the pistol in his hand. The movement Emma felt from Mary on the back, caused Emma to ask.

"You okay Mom?"

"I'm fine, dear. Was just tempted to throw the French guy a zap!"

"Mother don't attract attention, I'm trying to get us away here, safely!"

"Hell the way you drive, one hopes for safety, Emma. You should really once everything is settled, get some lessons!"

Not replying now, Emma cast a glance and when she saw the French guy taking aim with his pistol, she accelerated all the more to make their getaway, even swerving across the road.

Within seconds when the French man, aimed his pistol, someone punched him in the stomach, leaving him to lie on the curb. His accomplice helped him up, the chauffer driven car, had pulled away. The French speaking man held his arm into the air calling for a taxi and then while the two men fell into its midst, he demanded.

"Follow that motor cycle!'

The cab driver half turned to stare at the French accented man. And then, without saying a word, pulled away.

"Hurry, we have got to get them, it's a matter of life and death!"

The cabbie followed the motorbike, it was a way ahead of them.

"Mother you have to hold onto me and the bar behind the seat at the back, there is a car coming straight for us and I'm going to do all I can now!"

Also adding, Emma ordered.

"You just read the signs and tell me which way to go!"

"Just be careful with the baby, dear!"

The cab drew up behind them. Before Emma could think, she opened up and accelerated on the handlebars and when the front tyre lifted into the air, she screamed.

"Hold on, Mother!"

All Mary could utter was.

"Oh my soul, what happened to the sweet Emma, I knew?"

In desperation she too cried.

"Emma I'm slipping!"

In the rear view mirror Emma saw that they had slipped the cab for the moment. Lying forward, even resting the baby bump onto the bike, Emma kept her gaze between the rear view mirror and the road before her. Mary fought only for a moment when sitting upright, against the wind before also lying lower, on top of the briefcase. When the cab again neared, Mary addressed the men, shouting.

"Have you got nothing better to do than chase two women on a bike?"

But her voice suddenly took on a high pitched tone when she informed, Emma.

"He's going to shoot, he is hanging from the window!"

"Hold on Mother!" She warned and steered the bike right across the road, accelerating even faster. It was moments before she allowed herself to breathe once the front wheel was safely back on the tar. But alas the man pointing the pistol was for some reason lying in the road.

"Shot Emma!"

Breathing a slight sigh of relief, did not stop Emma from driving any slower along the highway. The noise from the motorbike was thunderous and Mary had to shout above it.

"Honestly dear, you should really do something about your driving!"

It was to their horror when just a small way on, the motorbike slowed and came to a halt.

"What are you doing, Emma?"

"Nothing Mom, I think the fuel is used up!"

"Could you not have checked the gauge before, we go stealing a motorbike with a half empty tank.

Emma opened her mouth to say something but stopped.

"Well only one thing left to do. Start walking in

the hope of someone other than the French accented guys picking us up!"

"What were you thinking, telling me to leave my shoes in the waste bin?"

"Hardly would the stilettos have been appropriated for running and walking to make a getaway mother, trust me!"

It was sudden when the cab that had been driving the French accented guys, pulled up next to them. Emma's heart gave a lurch and Mary started to say to the cabbie.

"We cannot get any further, we cannot pursue this fight of yours, any longer. Are you satisfied now, we are stuck out in the middle of who the hell, knows where?"

"Wow, Ma'am!" The cab driver started explaining, while holding up his hands, in defense.

"I'm on your side now. When I saw it was two women that those men were treating so disrespectfully, I decided to come over to your side!"

With an air, Mary insisted.

"Well, where are they?"

"When the one pointed the gun at you, I knew he was leaning out too far, so I swerved, he fell out. When the other got out to help him, I drove away. Now I'm at the service of you two lovely ladies!"

While climbing in to the comfort of the back seat of the cab, Mary complained saying.

"I don't know if I'm ever going to walk properly again!"

"Why mother?"

"Being forced in half for that length of time, on a saddle!"

Emma giggled. The driver was still talking.

"I was thinking to myself. How can two men want to kill two women on a motorbike? I would be an accomplice, had I assisted them. So I swerved and came to help you!"

The road further from the comfort of the cab back seat, seemed interesting when reaching the lights of Caesar's Palace, Mary raved saying, and it looked like being in America. It was the cabbie that suggested that they stop on there and allow him to show them the beauty of the entertainment house.

"It lives 24 hours of the day, all week!"

As usual Mary being a social butterfly thought it a brilliant idea and when the cabbie insisted that they would be starting a new fashion, by going barefoot.

"We have the time so a couple of good hours of entertainment cannot do any harm!"

Something was troubling Emma and she made no secret of it.

"Those two men are somehow going to follow us!"

And later in the evening, while walking at the gambling machines, Emma noticed both men, standing scouring the amusement hall.

"Quick, they are here!"

"Who Dear?"

"The two men. We have to get out of here and you Mr. Cabbie, they are going to shoot you with us, so let us go!"

Now having to sneak out and not be noticed by the two men, Mary asked the cabbie.

"How the heck could they have got here?"

It was on being outside among the cars that the cabbie pointed and said.

"O, O!"

Emma added.

"There's the motorbike. They must have got petrol!"

Cabbie called.

"This way Emma, the cab is parked here!"

But Emma went up to the motorbike and while saying.

"I'll just take the keys so they cannot go further!"

When she had tucked the keys safely away, she climbed into the cab and they left for the Lost City Hotel. There in the face of giant elephant and giraffe, among other animals in bronze, after waving the cab driver off, Emma whispered to Mary.

"Mom, you ought to go more carefully with the money. You just paid him enough to buy a new cab!"

"Oh my, I do wish they would stick to dollars through-out the globe!"

When they had booked into the hotel, the porter asked.

"Shall I get the luggage?"

He was stumped when the barefooted Emma, replied.

"Don't have any, thanks anyhow!"

When in their suit, Mary locked the briefcase away and ordered a bottle of champagne, saying.

"My gosh, that was some hell drive, Emma. You should really get lessons. I could have been killed!"

Emma broke out laughing.

"What are you laughing at, dear?"

"Oh mother look at yourself in the mirror!"

Surprised at her own daughter laughing at her, she turned to stare at herself in the mirror. And then while breaking out into laughter Mary pointed at Emma.

"What?" She in turn asked.

"Look at your face. Gosh, South Africa has plenty of dust!"

"And we went to Caesars, looking like this!"

"And we booked in here, looking like this!"

The phone rang. It was not long when Mary was cooing to someone on the other side. When Mary ended the conversation, Emma asked.

"And that, mother?"

"It's the Sheik, just wanting to know how our stay is."

Mary also added.

"I forgot to tell you that we will have to get shoes as soonest, as we are going on a safari with a group tomorrow afternoon!"

Not having any business appointment yet, Mary and Emma did things together and when safely in the sightseeing jeep, later the afternoon, she sat close up to Emma, saying.

"Can't see how a wild animal, cannot pull one

from these jeeps but anyhow, I think, sitting right here in the middle, I am giving the animal, plenty of choices, other than me!"

In the same breath, Mary cried.

"Oh Emma look, a lioness and her cubs!"

While saying this, Mary was stretching her neck so as not to miss anything but then the herd of springbok came across their path, she stayed quiet until they had disappeared into the distance, before she spoke.

"They are so graceful they jump almost as if clicking their heels in mid-air, in their get a way!"

The guide steered the jeep to where the bird watch, hide out, was. When the tourists had all stepped out and were about to enter the long enclosed passageway made of sticks, Mary pointed and whispered.

"Leopard, he's close and we are not protected!"

The guide saw Mary's panic and explained.

"Take note that the leopard is walking up and down, yes, he is watching us. It feels scary to be so close to being attacked. Look a little closer and see that there is electric fencing all around the area where we are allowed to leave the jeep. We are protected from being his meal!"

The guide spoke again.

"Now if you will all speak in hushed tones, the birds will not suspect that we are intruding on their privacy!"

The group disappeared into the naturally made passageway that led down to the dam. There in a room made of wood, the tourists were able to lookout through small holes, onto the birds, sitting a few meters from them. On the outskirt of the picturesque dam, Mary saw a huge dried tree, it stood reflecting into the crystal waters beneath. Within the trees open arms it beheld as birds chattered and communed, basking in the sunlight, oblivious of the closeness, of the vibrations of a human being, in their space. On the branches of the tree, a Kingfisher rested while his eyes skimmed the surface of the waters for the movement of a fish. In the crisp of bluest heaven, far above eons of mountains, the Fish eagle cried, sending out his Ode. Finding herself in awe by the very experience, Mary had an unexpected desire, a needing for what she experienced as a child. Her father would cruelly beat her and kick her, until she felt like a broken doll. She learned to go inside of herself, searching for that loneliness of her soul, needing it, wanting to embrace it, wanting to find the broken child within, to still her pain and kiss her heartache, to cherish her and hold her within the palm of a hand, protecting her. Now at this point in time, when looking out to where only nature abounds and her father could not hurt her, Mary knew she could stand whole and that from such a simple experience as today.

It was only in a long while before the guide drove the jeep into an encampment, when the warden opened a gate, the guide instructed.

"We are going into the lions' area now and I suggest that everyone keep arms and legs from hanging out and don't provoke the animals!"

Snuggling up to Emma now Mary held onto her arm, she whispered.

"The people sitting on the far row are more in danger than we are?"

Once inside the encampment, the jeep stopped for the first gate to close and then the second gate opened. Here, lion laying beneath trees, among the dry grass, stared as they in the jeep, drove slowly by. Everyone on board the jeep rose to see when a lion was ripping at pieces of raw meat, pulled from a carcass.

"We are now where they are being fed. Can you imagine how many carcasses it takes in a year, to keep the lions satisfied? You see if they are hungry, they will be attacking every animal out there, so they get fed in here and go out into the open with full tummies!"

The crowd laughed. A lion neared. He seemed aggressive while he strutted as if owning the place. When he got to the jeep, he jumped up onto his hind legs, with his front paws onto the lower bonnet of the jeep. The people in the jeep let out a deep uncertain sound.

The guide spoke.

"Down girl!" And started to reverse the jeep slowly.

The guide grinned.

"Not that down girl means anything to them!"

The lion now bit at the turning wheels of the jeep but a lioness appeared, carrying her chunk of raw meat and the lion turned his attention away from the jeep.

The guide spoke on.

"Can you imagine how strong that jawbone is, ripping the flesh at such force!"

Someone in the jeep spoke.

"Have they attacked anyone?"

"There was one attack on someone that got out of the vehicle. He had been drinking and was playing a game with his buddies to show how brave he was in the face of danger. A lion did chase him and out ran him, so he was attacked. You know when a lion attacks they go for the jugular vein. The person was running with his back to the lion and was killed instantly. Need I say more?"

Mary spoke now, so only Emma could hear.

"Well, that was another first experience that I won't be doing again. I mean endangering my life to see fully grown lion feeding. What the human won't do to entertain himself.

"Mom, you're so funny, but I love you so much!" Emma stated through her laughter.

The tour guide took the group to the very top of a hill and there in the sunset, they feasted on traditional babotie and rice with mealie fritters and champagne.

"This is absolutely divine!" Emma insisted, turning back for seconds.

It was on leaving the safari jeep, which the guide reminded.

"Balloon drive over the resort, at the crack of dawn. See you all then!"

And at the crack of dawn, it was Mary, telling Emma.

"I cannot get my eyes to stay open but here we

are, waiting for the hot air balloon to take off. Clinging on for dear life, Emma stood against the basket area in the balloon. Mary was nervous and placed her hand onto Emma's arm for extra support, but once the bluest flame was spitting its energy into the balloon, it rose, moving swiftly up into the air and on staring down at the scene playing out below, one realized the magnificence of the moment and stayed quiet. When the flame of the hot air balloon was not being fired, one could only hear the wind and the movement of the animals below. When frightened by the unexplained movement just above them it would send them to seek safety. When gliding over the crater made in the earth, Mary was still holding onto Emma's arm but now, in fear, with an almost pinching grip. It seemed that all breathed a sigh of relief, when the basket was safely back on the ground. Champagne was served and a breakfast of cheese grillers, mushrooms and French toast and watermelon balls followed. When again in their suite, Mary flopped onto the bed, saying.

"I'm too clapped to do business!"

"You had better go easy on the Champagne, Mom!"

Emma also suggested.

"Let's take a walk down to the Sea of Waves?"

"I'm too tired, you go!"

"I'm not going alone Mom, even if I carry you out here!"

"Oh Emma, alright then!"

It was a short walk and Mary was taken in with all the tourists around and the décor of the place.

"Such magnificence of the statues, one cannot fathom how anyone could in the middle of nowhere, have thought of placing this wondrous experience!"

She also added.

"The gardens are really something. Sol Kerzner knew his story to have designed such a place!"

It was in their walk that one could see the tall green minarets appearing between the top of the trees and before you knew it, you were standing on the bridge that you had to cross to get to where the Sea was. And when hardly onto the bridge, it started moving and rumbling, like of old. Mary ran to get to the other side, saying.

"Hurry Emma!"

"It's not dangerous Mom, just special effects!"

"Oh, feel something like in King Arthur's days!"

On turning back the bridge was smoking at places and Mary laughed, now enthusing.

"It seemed so real!"

Through the air laughter came, as in the blue waters before them, people were playing among the man made waves. Children were screeching in delight. When Emma and Mary followed the path back toward the hotel, a rope bridge greeted them.

"Oh heck you are not getting me on that thing!" Mary insisted.

"No other way back Mom!" Emma joked, saying while walking onto the shaky bridge.

Mary took a few steps, squealing.

"Oh Emma, I can't, come and fetch me!"

Standing on the bridge, a small way ahead of her mother, Emma was laughing.

"Mom, with the baby being so close, I can't hold. You're making me laugh. Stop now!"

But Mary was serious, she could not budge although having walked a tiny way onto the bridge. She was placing footstep for footstep and moving at a slow pace when Emma now turned and while holding onto the sides of the rope bridge, tread onto the wooden slats of its floor. The bridge was shaking and swinging. Slowly Emma reached Mary, who was now, quite irritated. Standing in front of her mother, Emma took her mother's hands, saying.

"Don't look down Mom, look at my eyes!"

And Emma started moving backwards on the bridge that was moving, threatening to swing, at their every move.

"Oh Emma once I'm off here you will never get me to do things like this, again!"

But Emma started laughing again and had to let go her mother's hands and wait for the moment of laughter to pass, the bridge was shaking and Mary insisted on running ahead though leaning skew, the last paces saying.

"I haven't time for your laughing now!"

Insisting on going back to the hotel she immediately ordered a bottle of Champagne, stating.

"First a hell ride to get here and then this, it's enough to drive anyone to drink!"

It was when the Guide called Mary and invited for them to go into town for some shopping that Mary felt safe enough and gave Emma some money, saying.

"I'll pay you to go with me, for shopping!"

Not refusing such offer, it was shortly when Emma sat on the jeep a way from Mary to do the shopping. Mary complained aloud.

"Geez are there no tar roads, here?"

The guide had stopped at a single storey building with plenty of small shops and Mary asked.

"A spaza, what's that?"

"It's a name for a shop selling emergency foods!"

"This is primitive, to what I was expecting!"

"Mom, this is rural area and they only buy what is needed!"

"Well in that case I'm not even getting out of the jeep!"

But Mary went on to say.

"See if they have some Swiss chocolate, Emma!"

"Mother, these people will probably never see Swiss chocolate in their lives. They just don't even sell much chocolate out here!"

"Well, I expect you to give my money I paid you for the shopping today, back!"

Laughing aloud now, Emma exclaimed.

"Oh no, you don't. You did not make any conditions to the money. Thanks Mom!"

And Emma flashed the 20 Dollars at her.

"Well, this is turning into a nightmare for me!" Mary disclosed not knowing what was about to happen.

For Emma, it was great doing shopping at The Lost City, for one it was close by, within the building, most of all there was a variety of shops and entertainment. Mary had been doing business most of the time, promising.

"As soon as I clinch this deal, it will be holiday time, for you and me!"

However, Mary kept busy with the deal and stayed in a bad mood throughout. For Emma, while browsing through the clothing shops, rather than being at the gambling machines, she tried and fitted every garment that she wanted and bought more than enough. It was only when Emma felt the pistol in her back that she stopped in her tracks but at each of her elbows stood suddenly a strong pair of hands, forcing her outside and into a car parked in the driveway. The two French accented men tried to sound jovial when they chatted, so as not to attract attention to the fact that they were both holding onto Emma. Once in the car the driver made sure that the doors were automatically locked, before he set the engine in motion.

Half turning to see if anyone saw her leaving, she saw the highway filled with four lanes of speeding cars.

"What are you looking at? Do you think someone will follow you?" The one man asked.

"No!" She replied quickly.

"Where are you taking me and why is it that you don't leave me alone?"

"We need the baby!"

She did not know what to say but suggested.

"We have money in the suite, why do you not rather take that?"

The man sitting next to her was tapping at his head.

"Think Emma, think!" He stated while staring.

"The Brilliant is available immediately. Your mother was selling him for a Million Dollars, see now what I mean!"

"So where are you taking me?"

"We already have an offer on the table but now how is this for clever?"

"What?" She asked.

"We don't have to lug briefcases of money around, showing the world that we are doing deals and have money. No, we work with the Ice tears!"

The driver laughed saying.

"She does not know what the Ice Tears are?"

"Diamonds, my dear, uncut diamonds!"

"So where are we going?"

"I told you, we are going to exchange you and the Brilliant for diamonds and then one way out of the country!"

Her mind was racing while she debated to herself.

"I'm so tired of wondering where the heck and what the heck next!" And Emma stayed quiet for a long time.

The man sitting at the back with Emma started.

"Turn off here, George, this is the spaghetti junction, now go ahead for the Kimberley turnoff. We should be there in just under four hours!"

"We need some food and drink for the road!"

"There's a one stop just outside of, I'll stay with her and you can run in!"

The traffic was heavy from before the spaghetti junction, until at least the following half hour's traffic. It was bumper to bumper at places but once through after they had stopped for take away, the trip went well.

"The scenery here is flat and dull!"

"And that is when compared with the coast. We are not at the coast, in fact were at least 5 hour drive away!"

The drive made her tired but Emma was too afraid to close her eyes. It was on just reaching Kimberley, when she spoke for the first time, exclaiming.

"Oh gosh, look at those hundreds of pink flamingoes!"

The driver turned into the town which started with going around a circle. George commented.

"Geez! This is the cleanest place I have ever seen. No garbage lying around!"

A board pointed to the Mac Gregor museum and Mitch informed. "Do you see that board, goes to a very stately old, home that is now a museum?"

All in the car stayed quiet and he added.

"It is haunted, witnessed by many people who have seen the hauntings. I believe, there is even a horse without a head that sometimes runs through there!"

Not believing what she was hearing, Emma wondered what they talk about when they have an intelligent conversation.

"Horse without his head, running around!" She repeated and gave a small laugh.

They booked into the horse shoe motel and as they gave Emma the bed, the men slept on the couches. It was hot and even with the overhead fan going, the heat did not change much. She felt as if the little one tucked safely inside of her, was a small heater, radiating from the inside while on the outside, the Kimberley heat, played its part.

The following day, George and Mitch were kind enough to take Emma to a boutique called the Tom Cat in the city center, so she could get some clothing and shoes. As they drove through the very tidy town, the lawn in gardens around buildings was scorched yellow like that of corn. When they passed a building, George made a joke about it, saying.

"The Diamond house, this is where my next job is going to be!"

He told of friends that worked there.

"Both the young husband and his wife worked there. She was pretty decent and ended up working where the diamonds get weighed and she had a trusted reputation, thus did after years not need to be screened. When the hubby kept pushing for her, to bring out a diamond, to stop his nagging and moods, she did. In her mouth!"

"How were they caught?"

"The same as everyone that does things like that, they started spending lavishly and living it up!"

"What happened to them?"

"Jail sentences!"

While looking at his watch, George stated.

"Let's give Eldo a ring and hear when he can see us?"

Turning to watch Emma while Mitch was making the arrangements, George was perspiring.

"Geez. It's hot out here!"

Mitch threw himself into the back of the car saying. We must meet him at the Kimberley Mine within the next half hour. There is a tourist group meeting and he will be among them!"

When they arrived at the old mine, George inspected the yester year train coaches and laughed, calling.

"Come and look at this. The original old dining coaches of the day when they were mining this big hole!"

"Where's the big hole?"

Emma was walking between them and piped up.

"You don't need to hang onto me, I've got nowhere to go!"

While standing on the ledge of the lookout over

the old mine, one could not help but stare into its depths that seemed to pull your being like a magnet, drawing one down into the deep green waters. Far below the lookout, a bird was circling, flirting far above the green pit. Around its sides, ledges of pathways circled up as the pans of yesteryear brought up the ground to be searched for the diamond. The iced tears.

"Wow. It's deep!"

"And wide!"

It was at the museum, where the largest diamond ever found was on display that a voice stood suddenly behind George and said.

"I have had a good look at the merchandise, I'm impressed but your price is a bit high. I will speak to my partner and be in contact with you within the next 24 hours!"

The two men nodded in hope of Emma being sold and off their hands. It was when Mitch put his head close to the showcase with the pink diamonds in, that on bumping his head, he exclaimed.

"Did you see the price of a Rose Cut diamond, shit, who the hell can afford that?"

His phone rang, he walked away out of hearing distance from Emma.

"Yes!"

"I see. It will be in order!"

"See then!"

He turned to George, we need to pick up uncut stones for Mademoiselle. It has been arranged.

"When and where?"

Today on a small holding near the place where we came into Kimberley!"

On their way, Mitch reminded George.

"The dame's about to give birth, slow down on these dusty rocky roads, man!"

Emma turned and stared out of the window, wondering where she would be if the baby decided at this moment to be born. She thought of Anton and longed for the safety of his arms. It was arriving at the small holding where the two were to collect the stones that she drew in her breath at the beauty of the gardens around here when just a small way away, a dry city amid earthly colors where it looked as if nothing green was to grow, survived. The lawns of the home were laid out and lush. The house was stately and on entering one could only wonder what love and dedication had gone into the interior and decoration. When the men were summoned to the study, she walked between them, whispering.

"No chance of escape here!"

It was when they were all seated that the owner poured the small bag of rough stones into a tray. Emma wondered what they really were, because they did not look like diamonds. When the men in turn pinched the eyeglass to their eyes and stared at the beauty of a stone in the light, Emma knew that this was an illegal operation. The owner showed as the stones played, reflecting rainbows of light onto paper. The men whistled in awe and closed the bag of stones. The owner spoke first.

"Mademoiselle made the deposit, the stones are yours!"

As they rose to leave, sirens sounded and the diamond squad stopped them from leaving. Headed between a convoy of police cars, they were taken to the headquarters. Mitch warned.

"Mademoiselle warned when in trouble she is not taking no blame for whatever it is, we stand alone!"

Emma was sitting quietly in the back of the car but her heart was beating like a jungle drum.

"Mademoiselle has warned us over and over. The job is risky and if things go wrong, she isn't sticking out her neck for any of us!"

In the small office where they were taken,

Emma wondered what she was supposed to do. Mitch warned her.

"If you talk now, we spill the beans!"

Sitting quietly Emma watched as the diamonds were taken from the men. Each was inspected thoroughly and put aside and another was taken and the same procedure was repeated till all the diamonds were done and back in the bag.

The Officer gave the bag back to Mitch, saying.

"Congratulations you have just bought yourself fake diamonds. You are not guilty of being in possession of uncut diamonds. You may leave!"

The policemen were laughing aloud now and Mitch was humiliated and angry.

All the way home the men stayed quiet wondering, what the hell they were going to tell Mademoiselle.

It was the following day when going to the Kimberley Mining Town, to meet the lead they got.

"He wants to buy the Brilliant!" George stated while staring into the coaches of trains from days gone by, Emma could only imagine how the elite of that day must have enjoyed the treatment they got, judging by the dining saloon and the luxury of the utensils and décor. It was when standing in a group, watching the demonstration of diamonds being mined, that a voice spoke next to Emma. He addressed Mitch and George saying.

"The money for the woman and the Brilliant has been deposited by Electronic transfer. We shall wait and when you give the nod that all is okay, the girl and I will depart!"

Her heart was saddened, Emma thought of Anton and she could not believe that this was happening to her. She thought of their plans to marry after the baby was born in the summer. She wanted to cry when thinking that she would never feel Anton's lips on hers again. Emma knew not to go against their plans, she did not want to endanger the baby's life and she obeyed their orders.

When Mitch and George, who were staring at their phones, now looked up, they waited a moment and when Mitch said.

"Yes, Mademoiselle!" He nodded.

It was George that instructed, Emma.

"Go with the client and you will be well looked after. You and the Brilliant!"

She did not look up at the client but heard George say to Mitch.

"I reckon us having sold the woman and the Brilliant will not have our throats slit for bringing back fake diamonds.

When the client placed his hand onto Emma's arm, she did not fight it. She sat in the front seat of the vehicle, with him, the driver and they drove in silence. The car headed for the Barkly West road and after travelling for a half hour, he invited her.

"Come and see the view. This is a volcanic vein. Can you see it looks as if the earth has cracked open, exposing this beauty and treasure?"

She stayed quiet but took a footstep closer to look over the massive crack in the earth. The ground on the sides led quite a way to its lower bed, where crystal clear water flowed. The man who had bought her, reached out, taking her hand in his and to Emma it felt strangely familiar. She looked up at him for the first time and recognized his gentle brown eyes and when his lips touched hers, she whispered.

"Anton!"

"I told you, I was by you every step of the way!"

He removed the dark moustache and took the dark hair piece off. Anton turned back to the car and from the boot, fetched a blanket and a basket.

When he was back, he reached out and took Emma's hand into his, helping her all the while to walk down the pathways that led to the water. When reaching the bottom, Anton while removing his clothing, demanded.

"Excuse me while I make myself comfortable!"

She squealed with laughter saying.

"You are in your boxers!"

"Wait here and you will see why!" He answered.

He carried the basket, the blanket and his clothing high, near his shoulders and waded into the water to get across. He left it all on the island. When he came back, he climbed out of the water and without saying a word, lifted Emma onto a piggy back ride while holding her legs at each of his sides.

Emma was screeching with laughter that she was hanging over backwards and Anton too laughing now, demanded.

"You're making me laugh too much, I cannot move!"

Hardly had she promised to stop laughing, when they both fell into the water. He reached for her asking.

"Are you okay?"

She could not talk as she was still in stitches. But suddenly when feeling the closeness of each other, Anton disclosed.

"I love you and missed you so much it is difficult being apart from you now a days, my love!"

Emma reached toward him and once in his arms, said.

"I've missed you so much, my love!"

He assured her.

"Soon we are to be married and then there will be no separations between us. I love you my bride to be!"

In the water he unloosed her dress throwing it to land on the small island. He drank in the perfection of her youth, while smoothing softly down over her and at her thigh held her to him. It was when he ran his tongue over her lips, she giggled declaring.

"I love your wild and weird ways!"

"Sioux blood, darling!"

She giggled. A dove called up in the trees, somewhere. While their eyes were locked in embrace, she was bewitched by his untamed love, but safe in it. Her arms were reached around his neck and while weightless in the water, slipping down within his grip, she his irrational need, within the icy overpowering water, she whispered.

"I want this moment to last forever!"

He pulled her to him, Anton's kiss was demanding and when his body moved against hers, he kissed her neck, even to her inner thigh. His mouth searched, their eyes spoke and when it felt like her heart had become crystal, she stood with him on heights where it broke giving a release from her inner being. A release that had fought to possess, to love, to be loved and then in submission, fallen, triumphing in their enigma.

When out of the water and on the small island, Anton threw down the thick eiderdown for comfort, inviting.

"Come and relax, I think you and the little one

have been tested far enough, in taking strain!”

Unpacking the food basket, he made sure that Emma again was eating nourishing food and juice. He also joked.

“And if you eat all your healthy food, I brought you this along, from the Swiss Alps!”

“Yay, my favorite chocolate, yay. Not going to have food, need chocolate for strength first!”

He laughed aloud informing.

“That is the Emma I know!” And he passed her the chocolate.

It was long after they had finished eating that while Emma lay next to Anton on the blanket, she stroked over the warmth of his back muscles.

“I love the way your muscles ripple when you move. I love your strength. You know, I love you, do you?”

He turned his face to her whispering.

“My word, but you are beautiful!” He stared at her before him with much urgency in his voice, whispered.

“No, I have forgotten if you love me. Show me!”

She giggled and slapped his bare butt.

It was at the end of the day when Anton started by saying.

“Emma, I am taking you back to your mother, but I will be in disguise, still following you everywhere!”

“Why would you do that?”

“I have a story to tell you. What I’m going to tell

might shock you but I am here for you and it will never change my love for you!"

It was already sunset when they reached the car and Anton spoke of his plans.

"Emma you know, I told you I will be with you everywhere, though in disguise!"

She nodded and he spoke.

"You know your mother is selling the Jagirremi Formula and with us following her moves we are catching the ones, who are dealing in crime!"

She nodded, saying.

"I know Anton!"

"Do you understand what a key player in this whole matter you are?"

She almost nodded but stared out of the window, while she spoke.

"Anton, my mother is very ill, she needs help and I cannot be asked to witness against her. I will not. I have to get my mother to get help!"

"Yes, I know and agree with you. No one expects you to witness against your mother. What we do need though is, that you help us for a few days so we can get the clients that are seeing her at the Lost City Hotel and then you are going to go back to the cabin!"

"They are not going to ask me to witness?"

"No, that I can promise you!"

"So now were going back to the Lost City Hotel?"

He nodded but added.

"I'm still at your side every step of the way and when I'm finished with my job, I will be heading back and we can be married when your arrangements are ready!"

"Your mother was in such a state with you disappearing, that she phoned Gavin for help immediately when you did not come home on that first night. Luckily he knew I was onto you all the way, though he did not tell her so. He just calmed her down and said to leave it in his hands. We will stay in the hotel and leave at first light back for The Lost City where you can meet up with your mother and I will be back in disguise. Gavin will let her know in the morning that you are on your way back!"

She laughed now when she asked.

"How did you pay for me when you bought me Anton?"

He laughed and explained.

"The Sheik allowed us to play a trick with the bank account of the woman who is in control of the two men. She is so desperate to buy the Serum that your father invented, that for a moment the money was deposited and then when they nodded for me to take my merchandise, the bank on working with us, pretended to realize their mistake and transferred it back!"

In the hotel room Anton ordered a light meal for

them and they watched the nature channel. He disclosed.

"We shall leave back at daybreak!"

Knowing so well that Mary was cornered, Kevin, spoke to Rick.

"The lead Philip gave through, was a definite one. She is here at the moment and seeing clients. The client that she thinks she has, however is against this selling of Emma and her baby. My Emma is here, we have to take her back with us, to safety and bring Mary now to justice finally!"

He also carried on to say.

"I have a really strong feeling that Mary has met her Moses in this client, I mean to have let the CIA know of her doing and that she is here!"

He also informed.

"Rick, you and I go for Mary as we have been, Emma at most times is with Mary but when she wanders off alone, I will split and follow her. Remember to stay well hidden, even if we are wearing disguises. We will later meet with the disguise artist in our suite as Philip has arranged. Be careful at all times, it could still prove to be risky, Mary knows us well. Emma must not be traumatized now!"

The disguise artist was waiting and they changed in the hotel suite and set out immediately, for the sake of Emma.

"Time is running out, the baby is due soon!" Kevin breathed.

Later, while standing in the curio shop, Kevin turned and suddenly found himself a few meters from Mary. It was almost as if he could reach out and touch her.

It was while Mary was paying for the item, she had bought, and that Kevin wondered where Emma was…

29 started with my grandfather and 8 with my mother… and now I'm 50 and I told you two stories. The third one is all three combined and this one is the third one….50

The people around were now captured with this revelation. Chrystal said softly…

"Tell them about Emma."

We bought Emma back to make it look like the transaction of the century for Mary. Mary was in the seventh heaven because she finally got her money for the Brilliant. It was a team of brilliance who got her to the plane. Everything went according to plan. One hundred percent. As soon as Emma boarded the plane to be flown to a certain destination die two pilots in the plane had their job to do. To deliver Emma back home. They gave her a new passport a new name and took off from OR Thambo airport in South-Africa and delivered her in America. She had a baby boy and called him a name of their choice…never the "brilliant." A blessing from an experiment and so many things that can follow. Eddy, as for Emma, also got a new name and new home. Most wonderful place to grow up as a normal kid. They are still alive and they will be here shortly. I call them now Mom and Dad.

One of the audience put up his hand and asked. "Who are you then?"
"I'm 50 years old today and as a celebration of my life I'm releasing the book "50" as a story about 29 and 8 combined and then this book will be just "50"
The guy in the audience was still not satisfied and said it straight.
"So you are the boy."
"Yes, I am." Never sold never away from Mom and Dad…up to my 21st birthday. They were very concerned that someone would know.

The guy asked.

"What is your name?"

My name is not important. My story is…with 29 we started a book which touched so many subjects and with 8 even more. What is important is what to tell you about 50. You can remember my by 50. I had a life like no other. Yes, I'm blessed with many gifts and blessings but never have I used them because I realized that I'm going to expose too many people in my stories. It can start with the new world order which is on everyone's lips. I can continue with mercury and with greed. Absolute greed for money and fame. That I could've had but I choose not to. I had the opportunities to do new things that could open so many more doors. But people these days don't want open doors. They rather keep it closed because the norm is better than to close it as to open it."

The guy continue…

"So you're him?"

"I'm 50 that is what is important and what else is important to see the characteristics behind the person you're dealing with. I've changed many people's lives and so do each one of you. Do it with grace and peace in your heart and you know that you meant something to someone. We all do. We cannot change the flow of nature but we can help it get the right balance back. We cannot change wars but we can talk about the people who we hurting in the process and what we're sowing and reaping at the end. What is the most important of it all is all the talents and blessings must be utilized properly and that is a big responsibility.

At my 21st birthday I took a bag and walked down the road and decided I want to change or help people in the right way. That was my path and it is still my path. At 22 I got my first degree, at 24 I got my honors, at 26 my masters and at 28 I was fortunate to be called doctor. So yes, I'm blessed and was blessed with a gift but my calling was to give it away. Never to hold it for myself but to help and to heal and to care.

I had a wonderful fulfilling life up till now. I care deeply about people and deeply about nature and deeply about children. It is them I form and them I give and them I bless and them I protect."

The guy again asked.

"What would you say to me if I want to change?"

"Be you. From the beginning to the end. Make up your mind if you want to follow a crowd or to stand out as one who really tried to balance the world we are in.   The world out there is changing and it is your responsibility to change it. That is my message to all. Use your gifts and blessings and help others to change. We need change, the world need to change and the only one who can do that is you. Just be the person you want to be. Don't do the wrong things, keep doing better. What you now sow, you will definitely reap one day. I'm 50 and reaping blessing after blessing and I am so grateful for that. What is my story for 50?

Blessings to you all, I've seen, I've heard, I've changed, I've lived, I tasted, I've smelled the roses and I still can contribute to the change I want to change. Yes, it's difficult, but come up with something that will be meaningful and will give you peace and humanity.

Someone asked…
"Where is Mary?"

Mary is okay, I made sure of that. She's at a place where she could be herself and enjoying the space she has.

Not big…but comfortable and good place to recover and heal and maybe one day…change back, but she's okay I made sure of that and she's safe.

Any other questions? There was none…however…

An old man came forward and put his hand on my shoulder, then an old lady came and put her hand on my shoulder. They said.

"This is our son and we are so proud of him. Now please each one of you, make your parents proud of you and live a life of tons of blessings and tons of love.

The end…

331

www.ingramcontent.com/pod-product-compliance
Lightning Source LLC
Chambersburg PA
CBHW070919260726
48661CB00003B/763